Hawaiian Legends
of
Tricksters and Riddlers

Hawaiian Legends
of
Tricksters and Riddlers

Vivian L. Thompson

Illustrated by **Patricia A. Wozniak**

A Kolowalu Book

University of Hawaii Press • Honolulu

In memory of
Marilyn Kahalewai
whose powerful drawings brought to life
the characters in
Hawaiian Myths of Earth, Sea, and Sky

Text copyright © 1969 by Vivian L. Thompson
Illustrations copyright © 1990 University of Hawaii Press

Library of Congress Catalog-in-Publication Data

Thompson, Vivian Laubach.
Hawaiian legends of tricksters and riddlers/Vivian L.
Thompson; illustrated by Patricia A. Wozniak.
    p.   cm. — (A Kolowalu book.)
Reprint. Originally published: New York: Holiday House,
1969.
Includes bibliographical references.
Summary: A collection of twelve Hawaiian tales about is-
land men who became tricksters in order to survive and others
who became riddlers in order to win a place in their society.
    ISBN 0-8248-1302-2 (alk. paper)
    1. Tales—Hawaii. [1. Folklore—Hawaii.] I. Wozniak,
Patricia A., ill. II. Title.
    PZ8.1.T3785Hau 1991
    398.2'09969'1—dc20   90-44432
                                               CIP
                                              AC

Development of the illustrations was supported in part
by Friends of the Library of Hawaii

University of Hawaii Press books are printed on acid-free
paper and meet the guidelines for permanence and durability
of the Council on Library Resources.

Contents

Acknowledgments

To the many generous people who helped me locate rare source material and check Hawaiian background, my warm thanks. A very special *mahalo a nui loa* to Elizabeth Ann Larsen, Nona Beamer, the late Dr. Donald D. Mitchell, Betty Babbitt, Keahiloa Braun, and Ann M. Pfaender.

Preface

TRICKSTERS AND RIDDLERS are found among the oldest and least-known of Hawaii's legends from earliest times when man became a trickster to survive; from later times when he became a riddler to win a place for himself.

The first voyagers to Hawaii saw land and sea filled with unknown terrors—evil spirits that could be overcome only by trickery. Their clashes with such terrors gave us the earliest trickster legends.

In time, new tales developed. Life was lived under strict kapu—law of the forbidden things—and the ruling class of chiefs held power of life and death over the common people. Not all such chiefs were just, not all benevolent. It was dangerous, even fatal, to rebel. So people took a mischievous delight in telling of ones who did rebel—fearless fellows who matched wits not only against

7

spirits and monsters but against chiefs and kings—lively trickster heroes.

Just as the trickster-against-spirit legend grew from primitive Hawaii, so the riddler legend grew from cultured Hawaii. As civilization advanced, stress was placed on mental as well as physical skills. The art of riddling came to rank with boxing, wrestling, spear-throwing, and other arts of war.

Riddling was seldom the simple matter of giving and answering riddles, as we know it today. It was more a matter of quick-witted debate which could take the form of imitating words and actions, making good a boast, matching and topping another's wit, engaging in complicated play on words, composing or memorizing long involved chants.

Such riddling required lengthy and intensive training and so was most often a chiefly accomplishment, for who but a chief had time to devote to such study, or authority to draw on the knowledge of others? But occasionally a commoner became a trained riddler in hope of improving his lot.

Riddling contests were conducted by definite rules, under skilled referees. Stakes were high. A man might risk all his possessions, his property, even his life, and once a challenge was accepted there was no way to withdraw. Success might bring undreamed-of rewards; failure might bring death.

Here, based on some of the earliest recorded versions, are some of those trickster and riddler legends retold for today's readers.

The Flying Spirits of Niihau

Early Hawaiians, to preserve their fishing grounds, observed strict kapu periods when certain fish could not be taken. When the kapu was lifted, competition was keen. Hardy fishermen, in great canoes hollowed from sturdy koa logs, paddled to distant waters—waters such as those off the desolate island of Niihau. Here, fish were abundant and competitors few—for a dreadful reason. . . .

IN THE DAYS when man-eating spirits roamed the islands, some fishermen of Kauai went out to fish off the shores of Niihau. How many? One, two, three, four, five. Their names? Ekahi, Elua, Ekolu, Eha, Elima.

All day they fished and their catch was a good one. When evening came they went ashore on the island of Niihau, cleaned, salted, and stored their catch and after their meal, lay down to sleep on the beach.

The sun rose on four fishermen. Elima had vanished. The other three turned to Ekahi, their leader.

"The spirits have eaten Elima! Let us leave! Who can say which of us will be next?"

Ekahi shook his head. "You speak nonsense. Elima has likely gone off for a little early shore fishing. No doubt we shall find him here waiting for us after our day's catch."

Again they fished all day. Again their catch was a good one. But when they came ashore there was no sign of Elima. The men talked little as they prepared their fish. Each kept his thoughts to himself. When their meal was over they lay down close together, and sleep was long in coming.

The third day dawned and but three fishermen remained. Eha had vanished.

"We must leave this evil place!" cried Ekolu. "If we had listened to Eha yesterday he would be with us today!"

"Ae. This is a dangerous spot," Ekahi admitted. "But we are fishermen. What fisherman ever had a safe life? We need opelu and this is the favorite feeding ground of opelu."

Elua considered this. "Ae. Our families depend upon this catch, and in two days the season ends. One more night then. But let us sleep offshore in the canoe."

So it was decided and so it was done. Another day's fishing, another good catch, and the evening meal eaten in their anchored canoe.

The three divided the night into watches. Ekahi took the first watch. It passed quietly. He woke Elua and lay down to sleep.

The second watch passed quietly. Elua woke Ekolu and stretched out, but slept only fitfully.

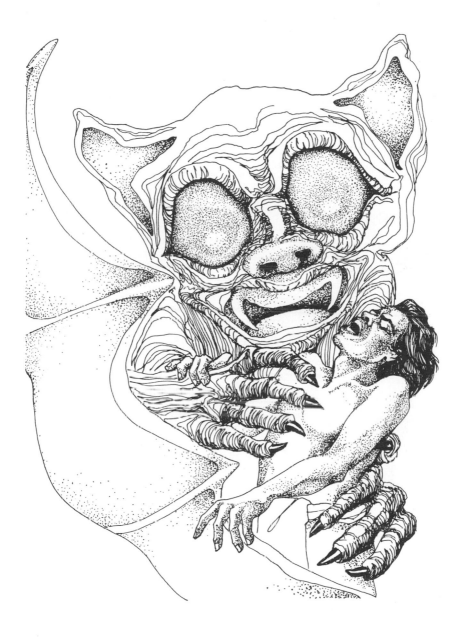

Just before daybreak, he and Ekahi woke at the sound of rushing wings and a muffled cry for help. They saw Ekolu struggling with a great, bat-like creature with pale, staring eyes.

They leaped to his aid. But auwe! One gulp and Ekolu had disappeared, eaten up by the spirit creature! With a flapping of wings it flew off into the morning mist.

"Turn home!" Elua cried. "Five came out, now but two remain! Better that two return than none!"

"Hold your paddle!" Ekahi ordered. "Return now and no man will dare fish here again. Without opelu all in our village could starve. We must destroy the wicked spirits that rule this island. Come, I have a plan."

Reluctantly, Elua went ashore with Ekahi. They saw no further sign of spirits. Through the long hot hours of the day, the two men labored between forest and beach, cutting and hauling, lashing and carving.

When evening came, a long house stood on the sand and inside, two wooden images, man-sized, with gleaming eyes of mussel shell.

Ekahi and Elua hid themselves and watched. The long lonely hours of the night dragged by. Their eyelids grew heavy and the two dozed.

They woke to the sound of voices. Two spirits were peering into the long house.

"The man-creatures have built themselves a sleeping place," said the first spirit. "But look! They sleep standing up!"

"Their eyes are open. They do not sleep," said the second spirit. "We must wait."

Time passed. In their hiding place, Ekahi and Elua crouched stiffly. Outside the long house, the spirits waited hungrily. Inside, the images stood with wide, staring eyes.

"We wait no longer!" cried the first spirit. "These men-creatures must sleep with their eyes open. Come!"

The spirits swooped into the long house and fell upon the wooden images.

"Aia! Tough and stringy, these two!" cried the first.

"Very hard, these men of Kauai!" cried the second.

Elua, while the spirits struggled, crept noiselessly to the door, tossed in a flaming torch, and ran. Ekahi launched the canoe. Swiftly they paddled away.

So perished the flying spirits of Niihau. So were the rich fishing grounds of Niihau made safe for the fishermen of Kauai.

The Weary Spirits of Lanai

To settlers in a strange new island home, food plants and trees could mean the difference between survival and starvation. So, to plant a breadfruit tree brought honor; to destroy one brought death. . . .

IN A TIME that was known as the golden age, the island of Maui was ruled by a great king. Many were the songs composed in his honor, for while other kings waged war to enlarge their kingdoms and bring glory to their names, he set his men to planting great groves of breadfruit trees so that all might have food in plenty and shelter from the hot sun.

When a son was born to the king and queen, there was great rejoicing. He was named Ka-ulu-laau, the Breadfruit Grove, to

14

honor the king. But the people fondly called him Ka-ulu. They brought gifts: leis of fragrant green maile, baskets of fruit, fish wrapped in ti leaves. The queen, who had made for the king the first feather cloak ever seen, made for Ka-ulu a matching shoulder cape. The king sought out all the male children born on his son's birthday and brought them to the palace to be Ka-ulu's companions.

But Ka-ulu grew up full of mischief. Time after time he led his companions into trouble, racing through newly-planted sweet potatoes, crushing young banana shoots, trampling tender taro plantings.

He and his playfellows became expert at a game played with arrows made of cane tassel stalks tipped with clay. Daily they gathered at a level clearing where each in turn sent his dart skimming along the ground to see whose would travel farthest.

One day, Ka-ulu and his friends arrived to find workmen digging up the clearing.

"Why do you dig here?" Ka-ulu demanded. "This is our playing ground!"

The workmen answered, "Your father the king ordered it. We are planting another breadfruit grove."

"Breadfruit! Breadfruit! Does nothing matter to my father but breadfruit?" Scowling, Ka-ulu led his companions away. That night, when all was dark, he slipped out and uprooted every young breadfruit cutting.

When the king heard of the damage, he ordered the culprit found and brought before him. Great was the sorrow of king and queen when guards brought in their own son.

The king spoke sternly. "You know well the penalty for destroying a breadfruit tree!"

"My husband! Not death for our only son!" the queen pleaded.

The king hesitated, then gave his verdict. "Banishment to the island of Lanai!"

The queen gasped. "But the island of Lanai is inhabited only by evil spirits! They will surely kill our son!"

The king would not be moved. "Since Ka-ulu is so fond of tricks, let him try his trickery on those spirits. If he is fortunate he may escape with his life."

The king left to give orders to the canoe-men who would carry Ka-ulu to the dreaded island. The queen bade her son a sorrowful farewell.

"Do not be sad, my mother," said Ka-ulu. "I shall find a way to outwit the evil spirits and make up for the wrong I have done. When you see a signal fire burning on the Lanai shore, you will know I have succeeded."

Ka-ulu stood on the desolate shore of Lanai, staring out to sea. In the distance lay the island of Maui. Nearby lay the barren island of Kahoolawe. In between, nothing but empty sea. His water gourd, food calabash, and sleeping mat lay piled at his feet. With a sigh he bent to pick them up. The sleeping mat unrolled and a bundle wrapped in damp ti leaves fell out . . . young taro and breadfruit plantings. His mother must have hidden them there. Ka-ulu, who had never expected to be glad to see a breadfruit tree, took them up gently.

He found a dry cave far up the beach near a quiet inlet and stowed his belongings there, then went inland and planted his taro and breadfruit. He was returning when he met four of the dreaded spirits. Their pale, unwinking eyes studied him greedily.

"Welcome to our island," said First Spirit. "Have you found a place to sleep tonight?"

"Mahalo. I have, thank you," said Ka-ulu. "Tonight I shall sleep in that patch of thick green vines."

The spirits looked at each other and smiled, knowing what vicious thorns grew on those vines.

That night, safe in his warm dry cave, Ka-ulu heard sharp cries from the spirits as they tramped through the thorny vines searching for him. Next morning, the spirits greeted him crossly.

"How did you sleep?" Second Spirit demanded.

"Very well indeed," Ka-ulu replied. "I heard some cries in the night but not enough to disturb me. Sea birds, no doubt. Tonight I shall sleep in that tall tree, away from the water."

Snug in his cave that night, Ka-ulu heard shouts and blows as the spirits struck at the tall tree, searching for him. Next morning, they greeted him sullenly.

"You slept well?" Third Spirit inquired.

"Very well, thank you," Ka-ulu replied. "The tree rocked a bit and the wind howled, but not enough to disturb me. Tonight I shall try that little cave down where the surf breaks."

That night, Ka-ulu, in his cave by the quiet inlet, could not even hear the spirits as they thrashed about in the caves near the big surf, hunting for him. Next morning, soaked with sea water, they spoke no greeting at all.

Ka-ulu said, "Such a restful sleep I had! The best so far. That is fortunate since I have important work to do today."

"What is this important work?" Third Spirit asked irritably.

"Cultivating my breadfruit," said Ka-ulu.

The spirits jeered. "No breadfruit grows on this island!"

"It grows here now," said Ka-ulu. "I planted it the day I arrived. When it bears fruit, I shall eat tasty breadfruit baked in the coals."

The spirits grew hungry at the thought. They moved closer with

threatening looks. "This is our island! The breadfruit belongs to us!" said one. "Show us where it grows!"

"Not so," said Ka-ulu. "No man shares the breadfruit but he who shares the work."

"Then show us what to do!" First Spirit ordered hungrily.

So Ka-ulu showed them. From sun-up to sun-down he kept the spirits busy clearing, weeding, and digging around his breadfruit plantings. The evening star shone down on a well-cultivated bread-fruit grove, four weary spirits, and a cheerful Ka-ulu.

Next morning, Ka-ulu was surprised to find eight spirits in place of four.

"We heard about your breadfruit," Eighth Spirit announced. "We have come for our share."

"Sorry. No work in the breadfruit grove today," said Ka-ulu.

"Why not?" demanded Seventh Spirit.

"Too much to be done in the taro patch," said Ka-ulu.

Sixth Spirit hooted. "No taro grows on this island!"

"It grows here now," said Ka-ulu. "I planted it the day I arrived. When my taro roots are ready for pulling, I shall eat freshly pounded poi."

The spirits' mouths began to water at the thought. They closed in on Ka-ulu. "This is our island! The taro belongs to us!" said Fifth Spirit. "Show us where it grows!"

"Not so!" cried the first four spirits. "No man shares the taro but he who shares the work!"

Ka-ulu nodded solemnly.

"Then show us what to do!" Eighth Spirit ordered greedily.

"Follow me," said Ka-ulu. The last four spirits got in line. The first four stretched out on the sand. Ka-ulu looked at them questioningly.

"We did our work yesterday!" they exclaimed.

"So you did," said Ka-ulu. "That was for the breadfruit, of course, so you will share in the breadfruit."

"But we want taro too!" they said.

There was no need for Ka-ulu to answer. The last four spirits answered for him. "No man shares the taro but he who shares the work!"

Sighing, the first four spirits joined the work party. From sun-up to sun-down Ka-ulu kept the spirits busy building terraces, carrying water, and flooding the young taro plants. The rising moon shone down on a well-flooded taro patch, eight weary spirits, and a smiling Ka-ulu.

The following morning, the number of spirits had increased to twelve. "We heard about your taro," Twelfth Spirit announced. "We have come for our share."

"Sorry. No work in the taro patch today," said Ka-ulu.

"Why not?" demanded Eleventh Spirit.

"Too much to be done on the fishpond," said Ka-ulu.

Tenth Spirit scoffed. "There is no fishpond on this island!"

"There will be one by sun-down today," Ka-ulu replied.

"Who needs a fishpond with a sea full of fish?" Ninth Spirit asked.

Ka-ulu shrugged. "No one who is willing to wait for the right season and the right weather and a day when the fish are biting. But with my own fishpond I shall have fresh-caught fish whenever I choose."

The spirits licked their lips at the thought. Each of the last four picked up a stone and moved menacingly toward Ka-ulu. "This is our island! The fish belong to us!" said Ninth Spirit.

"Not so!" cried the first eight spirits. "No man shares the fish but he who shares the work!"

Ka-ulu nodded gravely.

"Then show us what to do!" Tenth Spirit commanded impatiently.

"You have made a good beginning," said Ka-ulu. "Gather more stones like those you hold in your hands. Bigger ones. Heavier ones."

The last four spirits began gathering stones. The first eight sat down to rest. But not for long. The last four came toward them growling, "No man shares the fish but he who shares the work!"

Groaning, the first eight spirits joined the others.

From sun-up to sun-down, Ka-ulu kept the twelve spirits busy gathering stones, passing them along the line, building the walls of the fishpond. The evening breeze swept over a well-built fishpond, twelve weary spirits, and a satisfied Ka-ulu.

So the days slipped by and the barren island of Lanai became a green paradise. Never had the spirits been so well-fed—nor so weary. Ka-ulu overheard them talking one night.

"We finish one piece of work and this one thinks of another!" First Spirit complained.

"Before he came, we had no work to do!" Fifth Spirit growled.

"How much longer does this go on?" Ninth Spirit demanded.

"Be patient just a little longer," Twelfth Spirit coaxed. "The crops are flourishing. Soon we can do away with Ka-ulu and have all this fine food for ourselves!"

Grumbling, the spirits agreed. Unseen in the darkness, Ka-ulu grinned.

Next morning he called the spirits together. "The dry season is coming," he warned. "We must build a watercourse to bring water to our fields or our crops will surely die. Yesterday, high in the mountains, I found a stream. If we start today, clearing the stream bed and building walls, we can have the job finished in three months. Hurry! Get digging sticks and meet me here!"

Three months! Scowling, the twelve spirits went off for digging sticks. Ka-ulu, whistling, walked along the beach gathering driftwood.

Ten minutes passed. Fifteen. Twenty. Then Ka-ulu heard a great splashing. Across the channel toward the barren island of Kahoolawe, the twelve spirits were swimming as fast as they could swim.

Chuckling, Ka-ulu lighted the driftwood fire. While it burned down to a bed of coals he gathered his noonday meal. From his fishpond, a fat ama-ama . . . from his taro patch a plump taro root . . . from his breadfruit grove a ripe breadfruit. He buried these in the hot coals to bake.

Then he gathered more driftwood, armfuls of driftwood, enough to build a great signal fire—one that could be seen clearly from the Maui shore. For Ka-ulu by his trickery had rid the island of its evil spirits; by his planting had made amends for food destroyed. Now he could return to his father, his mother, and his companions in the shady breadfruit groves of Maui.

King of the Restless Sea

People who lived surrounded by the sea, dependent on its waters for food, travel, and relaxation, found sharks a very real menace. Hawaiians came to know them well—well enough to give them names and to plan ingenious ways to outwit them. . . .

PUNIA AND HIS mother sat on a cliff overlooking the water. His mother spoke sadly. "Beneath this cliff, Punia, lies the cave where your father died while gathering lobsters."

Punia nodded. "He was so fond of lobster, my father, and no one caught finer ones than he. I grow hungry for the taste of them. I shall dive down and get us some."

"Auwe!" his mother cried. "Would you die there too? That cave is still guarded by King of the Restless Sea and his ten shark follow-ers—the very ones who killed your father!"

"Hush, my mother. I have a plan," Punia whispered. He took a rock in his hand and said in a voice that carried clearly, "You want lobster, my mother? Now, while Shark King is sleeping I shall dive down over there to the left and be back with a fat lobster be-fore he wakes."

Punia threw his rock far to the left. Shark King and his hungry followers swirled after it. Punia dived straight down, got two fat lob-sters and was back on the cliff before the sharks returned.

He called down, "Mahalo, King of the Restless Sea. Thank you for sharing your fine lobsters with me! And you, Opunui, thank you for showing me how to get them!"

Shark King's glittering eyes moved along the line of ten sharks until they came to the one with the fat stomach. "Opunui," he said, "for showing Punia this trick, you shall die!"

Before Opunui could explain, the other nine sharks moved in and killed him.

Several days later, Punia again grew hungry for lobster. Return-ing to the same cliff, he said in a voice that carried clearly, "A fine day for lobster, my mother. This time I shall try that spot at the right."

He hurled his rock far to the right and while the sharks were gone, brought up two more fat lobsters. Then he called down, "Mahalo, King of the Restless Sea, thank you for sharing your lob-sters again! And you, Thin Tail, thank you for showing me the best spot!"

Before Shark King had finished saying, "Thin Tail, you die!" the other eight sharks had killed him.

So it went whenever Punia grew hungry for lobster, until at last,

Torn Fin, Crooked Jaw, Beady Eye, and the other five sharks all had been killed and only King of the Restless Sea was left. Punia knew that he must have a new trick to catch this wily one, so he made preparations.

First he got from his mother a large, closely-woven mat. Then he gathered two strong sticks, each about a yard long, a sharp shell, a small bag of sea salt, some kindling wood, and a pair of firesticks. Wrapping all these in a bundle, he fastened it to his back and returned to the spot above the Shark King's cave.

In a clear voice he said, "Do not fret, my mother. True, King of the Restless Sea is the most powerful of sharks but even if he should bite me, you know that I shall recover. Only if he should swallow me whole would I die and I shall take care that does not happen."

Shark King, lying in wait below, said, "Aia! This sly one shall not escape me this time!" When Punia dived, Shark King opened his great maw and sucked him in.

Before the cruel teeth could close upon him, Punia propped the great jaws open with his two strong sticks and, walking between them, wedged his large, closely-woven mat across the shark's throat to keep out the sea. Grazing his head, he made his way down into Shark King's opu. There, finding it wide and deep, he curled up for a nap.

Later, when he grew hungry, he rubbed his firesticks together and built a fire with his kindling wood. Then, scraping with his sharp shell, he gathered enough meat from the lining of the shark's opu to cook himself a fine meal.

Shark King, gasping with pain and coughing from the smoke, dived and surfaced, swam in frantic circles, darted out to sea and back toward shore, but he could not rid himself of his unwelcome guest. For seven days the struggle continued, while Shark King

grew weaker and thinner and Punia grew stronger and fatter.

On the eighth day Punia grew bored with his dull life and hearing the sound of breaking surf called out, "O Shark King, you may let me out here and I shall swim home."

Shark King kept on swimming.

Punia, making his voice tremble, pleaded. "O King of the Restless Sea, I beg of you, do not take me in to a strange beach! If evil spirits live there they will surely kill me!"

Shark King kept on swimming but his eyes gleamed faintly. With the last of his strength he swam to shore, ran aground, and there died.

Punia, grinning, started up the shark's throat to freedom. Suddenly he heard voices outside.

"See what we have found! Bring knives! Let us cut this monster up. Here is food aplenty!"

Punia crouched behind the matting in the shark's throat, listening. Were these evil spirits, in truth? There was but one way to find out. Tearing away the matting, he walked out of the great jaws.

Facing him on the beach stood a group of four men armed with sharp knives. Humans or spirits? Punia could not tell, for at sight of him they turned in panic and fled.

Puzzled, Punia scratched his head . . . and burst into laughter. He knew now what had frightened the strangers. His seven days of living in the shark's opu, grazing his head as he moved about, had worn away all his hair . . . and never before in Hawaii had anyone seen a bald man.

With a grin, Punia set out for home. In time, his hair would grow again. In time, his hunger for lobster would grow too, and in time, be satisfied. Now that King of the Restless Sea and his ten shark followers were dead, Punia and his mother could have fine fat lobsters whenever they pleased.

A Contest with Skillful Spirits

How could one overcome spirits? These awesome ones could take the form of a man, compete in his favorite sports, gobble him up in the wink of an eye. Strength and skill were not enough to defeat them. But if one had supernatural powers, or a very fierce god to protect him—what then? . . .

IT WAS A sad time in the district of Kohala. Evil spirits had destroyed the crops and the people were close to starvation. Only on the far side of the island, in dusty-eyed Kau where the spirits made their home, were food plants still growing, and these were closely guarded.

In desperation, the people of Kohala turned to a youth named Pupu, to save them. "There is no finer spearsman in the district,"

28

they said. "Did not the High Chief himself place a tuft of royal red feathers on your spear shaft to mark you as champion? If anyone can defeat these spirits and bring food plants back to Kohala, it is you."

Pupu welcomed the challenge and agreed to go. To spare what little food remained, he took none for his journey but carried his calabash of fishing gear to his canoe and set out.

Stroke . . . and rest. Stroke . . . and rest. Stroke . . . and rest. Stroke . . . and rest. He surged ahead hour after hour through the empty waters until he came at last upon a lone fisherman in a canoe.

Pupu rested his paddle and glided toward him. "What luck, my friend?" he asked softly.

"Auwe! All bad!" the fisherman replied ruefully. "Today, I who am called Small Barbed Hook for my fine catches, must return empty-handed."

"Perhaps not," said Pupu. He took a kukui nut from his calabash, chewed it, then spat into the water. Through the oily film he could see a school of silvery fish far below. "Drop your net deeper," he said.

Small Barbed Hook did so. His net soon filled to overflowing. When he had hauled in his catch he turned gratefully to Pupu. "You have helped me. Tell me how I can help you."

"I am Pupu of Kohala. I go to Kau to obtain food plants for my starving people, robbed by evil spirits. Can you tell me where these spirits may be found?"

Small Barbed Hook's tone was bitter. "Ae, they dwell beyond that point of land in what was my home before the evil ones arrived. They feed on the crops grown by my people while we exist on what we take from the sea, or starve."

Pupu looked thoughtful. "I have skill as a spearsman. You have knowledge of the district. Perhaps together we can defeat these evil spirits."

"Gladly will I join you," Small Barbed Hook answered. "But defeating them will not be easy. They too, are skillful spearsmen. If you approach them openly they will kill you. Only by trickery can they be outwitted."

Pupu smiled. "Then trickery we shall use. Come, let us head for shore. We have work to do."

As they beached their canoes and hid Small Barbed Hook's catch, Pupu explained his plan. "I will make the spirits believe I have supernatural powers and a fierce god to protect me. First, we will make such a god. Help me find wood."

They found a log of lightweight wili-wili wood and with his fishing knife Pupu carved a fierce, towering image. Small Barbed Hook found two gleaming pearl shells for staring eyes. Together they set the fearsome figure in the stern of Pupu's canoe.

The small fisherman looked troubled. "You do not know this district. The spirits have brought strange plants from far places. I fear they will trick you."

"Not so," Pupu answered. "The chants of my fierce god will tell me all I need to know."

"But how?"

Pupu pointed. "At the feet of my fierce god will stand a great covered basket and inside—one who knows the district well. Agreed?"

The face of Small Barbed Hook lighted. "Agreed!"

Together they gathered vines, together wove a great covered basket. Its mesh was small enough to hide one from sight, large enough to let one see out.

"Time to try our luck," said Pupu. Together they placed the basket at the feet of the image. Small Barbed Hook climbed inside.

"I can see clearly," he said. "Let us be on our way."

Pupu put the snug-fitting cover in place, pushed his canoe into the water, and climbed in.

Stroke . . . and rest. Stroke . . . and rest. The glowering image moved majestically out across the water and around the point of land.

In the distance, Pupu saw a group of spirits tossing spears along the beach. They stopped their game and came to the water's edge, spears in hand. Behind them, the people of the district labored, filling baskets with freshly-gathered crops.

A pale-eyed spirit called out in a challenging voice, "Who comes? Who comes?"

Pupu answered,

> "I come. Pupu of the Red Feather Tuft.
> I seek food for my god;
> My god of the pale, staring eyes.
> He has a great hunger."

The challenger stared at the image in the canoe, then took something from one of the baskets and held it up. "Here is food for your god," he cried.

Pupu faced his fierce god and bowed low. From inside the basket came Small Barbed Hook's whispered warning. "No! It is the poisonous bitter yam!"

Pupu turned toward shore and chanted:

> "My god tells me—
> One day to dig it,
> One day to stand it in water,
> One day to warm it in the sun,
> Then it sprouts.

But this is no food for my god!
This is poisonous—the bitter yam."

The spirit spokesman looked startled. He snatched two more objects from the baskets and held them up, one in each hand.

Pupu consulted his god again, then called:

"My god tells me—
Plant one in the dry upland,
It grows.
Plant one in the wet lowland,
It grows.
Wetland, dryland,
This is food for my god!
This is nourishing taro."

Another vegetable was held up and Pupu, after consulting his god, made answer:

"This too, is food for my god.
Dig it up, bake it.
When it is cooked,
My god will be pleased with it.
This is sweet yam,
A life-giving food."

The spirits murmured together, then their leader called, "Come ashore. Bring your canoe to the landing place where the water is calm."

"No!" came the whispered warning. "The place of rough water is the true landing place!"

Pupu swung his canoe away from the calm water and sent it surging through the tumbling surf. The spokesman frowned. "This one has supernatural powers. See how he knows the true landing place!"

The canoe shot through the foaming surf into the shallows. The spirits came running to meet it.

Pupu leaped out and held up a warning hand. "The stern end that bears my god is kapu! Only I may lift it!"

The spirits stole a wary glance at the fierce-eyed image and fell back. Pupu allowed two of them—a squint-eyed one and a snaggle-toothed one—to lift the bow as he took the stern. They eyed the canoe's contents greedily.

"A fine fishing calabash!" said Squint Eyes.

"What is in the great basket?" asked Snaggle Tooth.

Pupu answered curtly, "Something of great value. Something sacred to my god. We will speak no more of it."

When the canoe was set down on the beach, Pupu announced, "I can stay but a short while. Just long enough to get food for my powerful god."

A third spirit—one with a twisted mouth—said, "This powerful god of yours, if he is powerful, will protect you. Is it not so?"

"Ae. It is so."

"Then you would be willing to compete with us in a game of skill to win the food you seek?"

Pupu hesitated. "I would be willing, for the sake of my god. But I have little skill at games." He managed to sound worried. The spirits exchanged malicious glances.

Squint Eyes spoke up. "I challenge the stranger to a spear-hurling contest! Stakes, a basket of sweet yams against his calabash of fishing gear. Agreed?"

"Agreed!"

Short wooden spears were brought. A starting line was drawn in the damp sand.

"We throw for distance," said Squint Eyes. "The stranger may go first."

Pupu weighed the spear in his right hand, testing its balance. He stepped back a few yards, ran forward to the mark, and sent his spear whizzing. It flew through the air and came to rest a considerable distance down the beach.

Squint Eyes gave him a sour look and moved back for his turn. Three leaping steps forward, a powerful underhand movement, and his spear went skimming along the ground. It stopped far beyond Pupu's.

The spirits gave a gleeful shout. Pupu went to recover his spear. As he turned, he saw Squint Eyes take the fishing calabash from his canoe and reach out to lift the lid of the great basket.

"Hold!" Pupu cried. "The basket is sacred to my god! Touch it and you die!"

Squint Eyes leaped back but Snaggle Tooth broke in. "Another contest! Two baskets of yams against the stranger's basket!"

Pupu stood frozen. "I cannot wager the basket!" he declared. "I have told you, it is sacred to my god!"

Snaggle Tooth gave an evil grin. "Then your god will protect it. Take your place!"

Warily, Pupu took his place. Carefully he studied the course. These spirits were indeed skillful. He had lost on his first trial by throwing high. He must not lose, this time. Far more than an empty basket was at stake.

Running forward, Pupu threw his spear underhand and sent it hurtling a distance half again as far as the first time. Behind him, he heard Snaggle Tooth suck in his breath. He leaped aside just in time. A spear whistled past him and thudded into the sand—a few inches short of his own.

"Now I will take my winnings and be on my way," said Pupu.

"Not yet!" cried Twisted Mouth. "Enough of distance. I challenge you to a true contest of skill! Set up the markers!"

Squint Eyes and Snaggle Tooth ran down the beach and drove two stakes in the sand, a scant four inches apart.

Twisted Mouth handed Pupu three spears. "These must pass between the markers without touching either one. Best of three tries. Agreed?"

"Agreed," said Pupu. "For four baskets of wetland taro."

"Against your canoe!" cried Twisted Mouth.

Pupu stood speechless. If he lost the canoe, he lost his life and Small Barbed Hook's, as well.

"Has the stranger's god lost his appetite?" Twisted Mouth asked slyly.

"Not so. His hunger has increased," Pupu retorted. "He demands eight baskets of taro—four of wetland, four of dry. Agreed?"

This time, it was the spirit who hesitated.

"Has the native son lost his taste for a contest?" Pupu asked mockingly.

"Eight baskets," Twisted Mouth agreed, muttering. He took his place. He ran. He threw. His first shot scored. So did Pupu's.

Both threw their second spears. Both scored. Pupu felt the tension grow.

Twisted Mouth hurled his last spear. It struck the inner marker a glancing blow and set it quivering. The watching spirits groaned.

Slowly, Pupu took his place, estimated the distance, and threw. His spear sailed cleanly between the markers.

The spirits watched sullenly as Twisted Mouth led the way to the taro baskets. Snatching up a spear from the sand, he whirled and aimed it at Pupu's throat.

"Hold!" A weird, hollow voice broke the stillness. "Do no harm to Pupu of the Red Feather Tuft!"

The spirits spun about. Surely that voice had come from the fierce image in the canoe! They took one terrified glance and fled.

When they found courage to stop and look back, they saw the stranger's canoe moving swiftly out to sea. His fierce god still rode in the stern. The great basket still lay at his feet. With it stood three baskets of their best sweet yams and eight baskets of their finest taro. The canoe surged ahead as two men bent to the paddles —Pupu and a slight figure the stranger's powerful god had magically provided.

So it was that Pupu of the Red Feather Tuft brought food plants back to Kohala, and Small Barbed Hook who had helped him, found a new home.

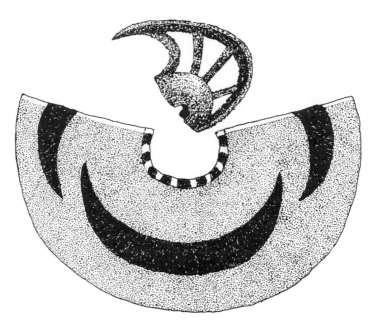

The Spirit Who Danced

In a culture where all men wore the malo—a loincloth made of kapa—kings and chiefs were distinguished by their elaborate feather cloaks and helmets. In times of war, such featherwork was a tempting prize. In times of peace, the same. . . .

CHIEF ALAKAI OF Kohala was going on a journey. He summoned his steward and said, "You are called Kupaa because you are steadfast and loyal to your chief. I leave you in charge while I am gone. See that my good name is maintained and my chiefly treasures kept safe."

Kupaa bowed. "O Chief, it shall be as you command."

The days went by and life went on in orderly fashion under

Kupaa's charge. Then came an unexpected visitor. A servant brought word to Kupaa.

"A stranger called Chief Wakaina has come to visit. He says he is a close friend of our chief."

Kupaa frowned. The name was strange to him. If this was a close friend of Chief Alakai, all honor must be shown him. But if he was an imposter, the chief's treasures were in danger. How was Kupaa to know?

He weighed the matter carefully. Then he chose a malo of fine, but not royal quality kapa and said to the servant, "Provide water for bathing and take this malo to the stranger with my compliments. Ask if he will join me in the evening meal when he has rested."

Later, Kupaa studied the stranger as he approached the eating house. He was tall, black-haired, handsome. He had a chiefly bearing but there was something disturbing about his eyes . . . something that brought a thoughtful look to Kupaa's face, as he went forward to greet him.

"May this humble servant welcome you in our chief's absence. Hele mai e ai. Come and eat."

The stranger ate with chiefly appetite. After a while he asked, "Is Alakai still fond of dancing? Many times in the past we have tried to outdo each other."

Kupaa nodded. "He is. You must be a gifted dancer to have competed with our chief. Perhaps you would honor us with a performance."

Wakaina bowed regally. "Wearing this fine malo you have provided, it will be a pleasure."

To the slapping accompaniment of the gourd drum, Wakaina danced a hearty foot-stamping hula and the people of the court applauded vigorously.

"Skillful indeed," said Kupaa as Wakaina finished.

"You are most kind," Wakaina replied. "I could perform a more intricate dance if I had come prepared. But alas, that dance requires a feather cape and I did not bring mine."

"Allow me to provide one," Kupaa offered graciously.

He excused himself and went to the chief's treasure house. Passing by the long golden cape of rare mamo feathers, and the short circular cape of red iiwi feathers, Kupaa chose a rectangular cape of black, white, and brown cock's feathers.

Wakaina donned the cape and danced a fine chest-beating hula to the rhythm of the coconut knee-drums. The people clapped and cheered.

"We are honored indeed, to have such a talented visitor," Kupaa observed. "Our chief will be sorry to have missed this rare treat."

"Ah, had I but brought my fine feather helmet, I would perform the Chief's Dance in my friend Alakai's honor. But when I travel I leave my treasured garments at home. Alakai does the same, no doubt," Wakaina finished smoothly.

Kupaa saw greed in the visitor's glance and felt a warning chill. He had identified the strange quality of those pale eyes.

"It would give me great pleasure to be able to tell our chief of such a dance in his honor. Let me provide a feather helmet," Kupaa suggested.

Back in the treasure house, Kupaa passed by the rich crescent-shaped helmet and the handsome wide-crested helmet of Chief Alakai and chose the mushroom-shaped head-dress of a lesser chief. On his way back, he murmured something to the servant, who nodded and disappeared into the woods.

Wakaina set the helmet on his head proudly. Borrowing sticks from one of the musicians, he began the stick-striking Chief's Dance. He was a gifted dancer. Of that there was no doubt.

Concentrating on the figures of the dance, Wakaina did not see the servant slip from the shadows and drop two large a-pe leaves behind him. Intent upon his clacking sticks, he danced on. Back and forth across the a-pe he moved, leaving no trace.

Kupaa nodded grimly. Wakaina was not only an imposter but a spirit! Only a spirit could tread upon the velvet-leaved a-pe and leave it unmarked.

Kupaa gave a sharp command. Wakaina's sticks halted in mid-air, his dancing stopped, and he turned angrily for an explanation of such discourtesy.

Kupaa raised his hand. From the shadows, the servant tossed a fruit of the puhala tree—the only talisman known to vanquish spirits—at the feet of Wakaina. With a shrill cry, the dancer vanished.

So, through the wisdom of Kupaa, the name of Chief Alakai was kept free of the shame of inhospitality and his chiefly treasures kept safe from the thievery of Wakaina, the spirit who danced.

Riddler on the Hill

Hawaiian chiefs used sports to train their men for war. Many chiefs were themselves skilled in such sports: bowling with the maika stone, racing on the swift holua sled, riding the heavy surfboard. Excellent training, these. Useful too, if a wily chief wished to rid himself of a rival. . . .

ONCE IN THE section of Oahu called Moana-lua, there lived a chief who was most vain. Whenever he appeared before his people, he watched to make sure that he was the center of attention.

One day he noticed an odd thing. His men all bowed low to the ground when he passed, but the women—especially the young women—stole glances from the corners of their eyes, at someone

43

behind him. Turning, he saw that it was Mekila the handsome, a fine young warrior in his train, to whom their eyes were drawn.

The chief was torn with jealousy and searched for a way to discredit his handsome young rival. Being known as an expert bowler, the chief challenged Mekila to a game of maika.

Mekila accepted. What else could he do?

The people gathered at the course to watch. The chief took his disc of black lava rock and sent it bowling a distance of thirty yards. The watchers clapped.

Mekila took his disc of white sandstone and sent it bowling a distance of forty yards. The watchers clapped and cheered. The chief congratulated Mekila briefly, and withdrew.

Next day the chief, an expert at sledding, challenged Mekila to a contest with the holua sled.

Mekila accepted. What choice had he?

The crowd followed to the steep holua course. An attendant carried the chief's favorite holua sled of highly-polished mamane wood, its runners gleaming with kukui nut oil. Mekila followed, carrying his own simple sled of uhi-uhi wood.

When all eyes were upon him, the chief picked up his sled, ran with it, and cast himself down. He flew over the course, traveling one hundred and fifty yards before he came to rest. The watchers shouted.

Mekila, on his sled, traveled one hundred and seventy yards. The watchers shouted and whistled. The chief congratulated Mekila coldly, and withdrew.

On the third day the chief, an expert surfer, challenged Mekila to a surfing contest. Mekila accepted.

All gathered at the beach to watch. The chief took his ten-foot board of glossy wili-wili wood, pushed it out into the sea and waited for a towering wave. He caught it, rose gracefully to his feet, and rode the wave straight in to shallow water. The watchers cheered.

Mekila took his well-worn seven-foot board of koa wood, caught a slanting wave and rode it twice the distance, landing in the shallows far down the beach. The watchers cheered and shouted, "Hana hou! Do it again!"

This time the chief did not wait to congratulate Mekila but stalked off angrily. How was he to get rid of this skillful young rival? There were no other fields in which the chief himself was expert. What should he do now? It was a riddle. . . .

A riddle! That was the answer. Riddling was a chiefly accomplishment. It was unlikely that Mekila had received any training in the art. Aia la! That was it!

But auwe! The chief himself was no riddler, having neither the time nor patience for it. Ah, but there was that wise man Paeli living in the mountains of Moana-lua. He could provide a tricky riddle!

The chief paid him a visit. Next day, he challenged Mekila to a riddling contest.

This time, Mekila hesitated. "O Chief, I know nothing of the art of riddling but if it is your wish, I will try."

"It is my wish," the chief replied curtly. "Here is the riddle:

> In the morning, four legs.
> At noon, two legs.
> At evening, three legs.

You have a week to find the answer. If you fail, death in the earth oven."

The watchers stood silent. The chief had not stated the terms of the contest until after Mekila had accepted the challenge. They knew now that the chief sought not a fair contest but a sure way to take Mekila's life. It was unjust but what could be done about it?

They could not defy their chief. They could not help Mekila find the answer.

Mekila set out bravely upon his quest. He traveled the length and breadth of the district. Of everyone he met he asked the same question. "What has four legs at morning, two legs at noon, three legs at evening?" None could answer.

Mikila studied the people he met. No answer. He studied the animals—the pig, dog, and rat. He studied the birds, the insects. Still no answer.

His time was nearly gone. On the morrow he must admit defeat and go to his death in the earth oven. Mekila started home. As he traveled the mountain path through Moana-lua he came upon old Paeli playing with his grandson.

"Have you found the answer?" Paeli asked.

Mekila shook his head wearily.

"Then hear me," said Paeli. "When you approach the chief, take care, for he seeks your life. I cannot give you the answer but this much I will tell you. The chief found his riddle here and here you will find the answer, if you give the matter careful thought. I can say no more." He called his grandson, waved to Mekila, then leaning on his cane, hobbled off.

Mekila started on his way, walking slowly, lost in thought. What had Paeli meant? There had been three persons in the group . . . and the riddle had three parts. He repeated the lines again and laughed aloud. Now he knew the answer!

On the following day as Mekila left his home, he saw crowds gathering. He saw too, his fellow warriors lined up in ranks before the chief's house. He could guess what their orders were. If he was to see another sun, he must find a way to answer the chief and still avoid his warriors.

Desperately Mekila looked about. Opposite the chief's house

stood a tall, flat-topped hill. Children were playing there now, wait-ing for the contest to begin. Mekila started toward them.

The chief's crier began his circle of the village. "Everyone is sum-moned to the chief's house for the riddling contest. Today Mekila must answer the chief's riddle or roast in the earth oven!"

A cloud of steam was already rising from the imu. The crier re-turned. There was no sign of Mekila.

"Sound the shell trumpet four times!" the chief ordered. "If Mekila does not come forth, my warriors shall find him and drag him to the imu!"

The conch shell sounded its low, sad call . . . once . . . twice . . . three times. . . . No sign of Mekila. It sounded its fourth and final summons. Before the echo died away, a shout came from the hilltop across from the chief's house. There stood Mekila.

"I have brought you an answer, O Chief," he called.

Then before the chief's startled eyes, Mekila began to act out the riddle's answer. He showed the sun coming up, and an infant crawl-ing on all fours. He showed the sun high overhead, and a young man walking straight and tall. He showed the sun going down, and an old man hobbling on a cane.

The people gave a glad shout, and no one shouted louder than Mekila's fellow warriors. The vain chief, hearing the sound, knew that he had best make no further plans against Mekila's life. He had been outwitted by the riddler on the hill.

Hog Child Plays Tricks

Who did not fear the kupua with his strange, baffling powers? Supernatural strength might be his, and the ability to change form. If he had also a fondness for pranks—Auwe! Such a one was Kamapuaa. . . .

WHEREVER WILD HOGS plunge through the upland forests strange tales of that one are still told. From the day of his birth he was different. So different that his elder brother Kahiki secretly brought the infant to the home of his grandmother in the hills.

"O Kupuna," he cried, "see this monstrous child born to my mother! Help us to hide him so no one may know of our disgrace."

Kupuna turned back the covering of the bundle in Kahiki's arms.

49

Inside lay a lusty man-child. Coarse bristles covered his body and he had the head of a hog.

Kupuna's eyes gleamed at the sight and she spoke angrily. "Stupid One! This is my grandson just as you are my grandson. He is a kupua and will grow to have rare powers. I shall call him Kamapuaa, Hog Child, and he will live here with me and grow to manhood."

Then Kupuna spread six sheets of fine kapa beneath the child for a bed, and six sheets of fine kapa above him for a cover, and sent Kahiki to prepare poi to feed him.

In the days that followed, Kamapuaa ate enormously, slept heavily, and grew rapidly. His brother Kahiki was kept busy from sun-up to sun-down providing food for him. At last, he rebelled.

"This hungry one gives me nothing but trouble!" he cried. "I am weary of providing taro for him! It is time he provided taro for us!"

Kamapuaa took his brother's words to heart. That night he changed into a black hog, rooted up the neighbor's taro, brought it home, and piled it at Kahiki's door.

When the neighbors found it there, they complained bitterly to Kahiki who called his younger brother to him and scolded, "Kamapuaa, your trickery has made great trouble for us with our neighbors. Now heed what I say! Never again will you steal from our neighbors!"

Kamapuaa took his brother's words to heart. He stole no more from his neighbors. He stole instead from the High Chief's royal hen house . . . four fat hens. Leaving two at Kahiki's door, he carried two off to the hillside to eat.

When Olopana the High Chief heard of it, he sent four men to take Kamapuaa. When they did not find him at his grandmother's home, they searched the hillside.

"Aia la!" cried one. "There he sits beside that rock, feasting on the High Chief's royal hens! Take him!"

The four raced up the hill. But when they reached the rock there was no man in sight. Only a big black hog with fierce white tusks.

"It is Kamapuaa the trickster!" cried the second. "Hen feathers still cling to his snout! Take him!"

They surrounded the black hog and moved in. But before they could take him, the hillside was covered with hogs: black ones, brown ones, spotted ones, and mottled ones. No man could capture them all, and who could say which one was Kamapuaa? Baffled, the chief's men turned back empty-handed.

When Kamapuaa returned home, he was met by his brother Kahiki, who roared, "Kamapuaa, your trickery has made great trouble for us with the High Chief! Now heed what I say! Never again will you steal hens from the High Chief's royal hen house!"

Kamapuaa took his brother's words to heart. He stole no more hens from the royal hen house. He stole instead the High Chief's sacred rooster.

When Olopana the High Chief heard of it, he sent eight men to take Kamapuaa, his brother, and his grandmother.

Kamapuaa heard them coming and helped his grandmother and brother run into the hills, with the High Chief's men close behind them.

Just as escape seemed near, they were brought to a sudden halt by a deep gorge directly in front of them. Behind them came the chief's men, closer . . . closer. . . .

"Surrender!" cried Kahiki. "There is no way to escape."

"There is," said Kamapuaa. "Help Kupuna across on my back." Turning into a great black hog, he stretched himself across the gorge and his grandmother and brother crossed safely to the other side.

But before Kamapuaa could leap away, the chief's men were upon him. They tied his feet together, slung him from a pole and carried him back in triumph to the High Chief.

Olopana ordered his men to place Kamapuaa, still in his hog form and still bound, upon the altar to be sacrificed. Then he called his kahuna to perform the sacred rites. When all was ready, the kahuna raised the sharp bone dagger for the fatal stroke.

"Wait!" cried Olopana. "I will kill this one myself!" Taking the dagger, he stood over Kamapuaa and said grimly, "Kamapuaa, your trickery has caused great trouble for me. Now heed what I say! Never again will Olopana, your High Chief, be troubled by your trickery!"

Before the dagger could fall, Kamapuaa broke his bonds, changed from hog form to man form, snatched the dagger, and slew his captor.

For Kamapuaa had taken the chief's words to heart, and never again would Olopana, his High Chief, be troubled by the trickery of Kamapuaa.

A Chiefess and a Riddle

In days now nearly forgotten, no man dared call anything his own. Chief took from commoner, high chief from chief, king from high chief. There was little to do but submit—unless one had great courage, rare skill, and a quick wit. Even then one might lose his life and all he held dear. . . .

ONCE ON THE beautiful island of Hawaii there lived a youth named Paka. Handsome he was, with glossy red-brown skin and back straight as a cliff. His uncles, both high chiefs, had raised him, training him in the chiefly arts of boxing, wrestling, spear-throwing and spear-dodging.

One uncle, Kii-who-goes, was a swift runner and a man of action.

54

The other, Kii-who-stays, was a man of thought, with power to see into the future.

When Paka was grown, Kii-who-stays said to his brother, "Paka should have a wife. Where shall we find a maiden worthy of him?"

Kii-who-goes replied, "I shall go in search of one, circling the island, if necessary," and he set out at once. Through the districts of Puna, Kau, and Hilo he ran. Through Hamakua and Kohala he ran. He saw many lovely maidens but in each he found some fault. He came at last to the district of Kona and there saw the young chiefess Makolea, daughter of the chief of that district, and she was as beautiful as the full moon.

Kii told her of his search for a wife for his foster son. Makolea answered, "Bring this Paka to me. If he is as worthy as you say, he shall be my husband."

Kii ran swiftly home with the good news. "I have found a wife for Paka! Let us leave at once for Kona!"

"Not so fast!" cried Kii-who-stays. "Let me see first what lies ahead." He closed his eyes and looked into the future, then spoke. "I foresee trouble. This lovely Makolea is promised to the King of Maui."

Kii-who-goes brushed aside his brother's words. "She said nothing of such a promise."

"This King of Maui is a champion spearsman," Kii-who-stays warned.

Paka broke in. "What matter, my uncles? Have you not trained me well in the use of the spear? What have I to fear from the King of Maui? Let us be on our way!"

So Paka and his uncles left their home and traveled to Kona. The young chiefess Makolea found Paka as worthy as his uncle had described him, and Paka found Makolea as beautiful as the full moon.

"Come, let us tell my father that we wish to marry," she said.

But her father, when he heard the news, spoke sorrowfully. "My daughter, gladly would I see you wed the man you love, but it cannot be. The King of Maui is a man of great power. He has threatened to make war on our people unless you become his wife. I, as chief of Kona, have given my word. You must marry the king to save our people."

"I cannot," said Makolea. "My love belongs to Paka."

At nightfall the matter was still unsettled. The chief provided food and a house for Paka and his uncles. The three, tired from their long journey, retired early.

Paka woke with the sun and hurried to the house of Makolea. At the door he found a serving woman with a message from Makolea. "My father has sent me off to the King of Maui. Paka, if you love me, come for me."

Paka hurried to the chief and begged for a canoe in which to go after Makolea. The chief shook his head. "If I send you after Makolea, it means war for my people. I cannot do this, my son."

Disconsolate, Paka walked along the shore, thinking of his lost Makolea. On a distant beach he came upon a canoe drawn high up on the sand. Joyfully he returned to his uncles with the news. That night, before the rising of the moon, the three made their way to that beach and set out in the canoe.

All night they paddled and in the morning landed on the Maui shore. Paka sent his swift-running uncle with a message to the king. "Paka of Hawaii has come to claim the maiden Makolea."

The King of Maui came out to meet Paka, carrying two spears, one in his right hand, one in his left. He drew himself up arrogantly and chanted:

> "Do you think to stand against my spear?
> My spear never misses!

Not a blade of grass!
Not an ant! Not a flea!
Then how should it miss the stranger?"

Confidently he hurled the spear in his right hand. But Paka moved slightly and caught the spear between his left arm and side and held it quivering.

The king stared at his spear, unable to believe his eyes. Then he shouted:

"What caused my spear to miss its mark?
Was it blown from its course by the southern wind?
No matter. My hand holds another spear.
This one shall feast on the stranger's flesh."

The king hurled the spear in his left hand. Again Paka moved slightly and caught the spear between his right arm and side and held it quivering.

When the king saw this he was terrified and thought to flee, but Paka moved swiftly. Once . . . twice . . . he threw, and the King of Maui dropped to the ground, killed by his own spears.

Then Paka found his beloved Makolea. His uncles arranged the ceremony, and Paka and Makolea became man and wife and settled down on the island of Maui for a time.

The King of Maui had been a most powerful man and news of his death spread quickly. Soon there came to the shores of Maui a royal canoe bringing a message from the King of Oahu. "Paka of Hawaii, I have heard of your fame. Come and be my adopted son and I will give you possession of the island of Oahu."

This was strange news indeed. Could it be a trap? What king would offer his power and land to a stranger? Paka consulted his uncle who looked into the future. Kii said, "I see a king offering a

golden feather cloak. I see land and fame and followers for you . . . and deep sorrow."

Paka shrugged. "If my beloved Makolea is with me, what sorrow can befall?" So Paka left in the royal canoe that waited for him, taking with him his wife Makolea, and his uncles.

When the royal canoe reached its destination, the King of Oahu came to meet the group. "Paka," he said, "I am growing old and have lost my taste for warfare and power. Be my adopted son and protect my island from warring chiefs." He took the golden feather cloak from his shoulders and placed it on Paka's. "Wear the king's cloak and rule in my place."

Paka was flattered by this sudden power and wealth. Who would not be? He enjoyed the lavish hospitality of the king and the admiration of his new subjects. Life was filled with unbelievable happiness.

He and Makolea were surfing with members of the court one day when their happiness came to a sudden end. Paka was riding his board at the King's Surf. Makolea, also an expert surfer, had gone down some distance to ride the Queen's Surf. As the sun dropped low in the sky, two of Makolea's attendants came running to Paka in great distress. Makolea had been carried out to sea by Ebb Tide and Flow Tide! Paka tried to question the women further, but they only sobbed more bitterly.

His Makolea drowned? Paka could not believe it. He ran to Queen's Surf and swam out searching. Back and forth he swam until the sky grew dark and he could no longer see. Then he made his way to shore and paced the beach in anguish. The words of his uncle rang in his ears: "I see land and fame and followers for you . . . and deep sorrow." His own words rose to haunt him. "If my beloved Makolea is with me, what sorrow can befall?"

As the evening star rose in the sky, his worried uncles came searching for him. When they heard the news, they too were filled with sorrow.

Kii-who-goes said, "Paka, my son, if the sea has taken Makolea it is the will of the gods. Come and rest. You cannot fight the gods."

But Kii-who-stays said, "Wait! I do not believe Makolea has drowned." He closed his eyes and murmured, "She is alive. She is being carried off by servants of the King of Kauai . . . and their names are Ebb Tide and Flow Tide!"

Then Paka was filled with joy and cried, "I must be on my way!"

But Kii-who-stays laid a restraining hand on Paka's shoulder. "Wait, my son," he said. "I see more. I see the King of Kauai standing between a grass house and a steaming oven . . . and death stands at his side."

Then Paka made answer. "I thank you, my uncles, for your loving concern, but I must go, and go alone. If the gods go with me, I shall bring Makolea back. If I do not return, you two must rule the island jointly."

At the first crowing of the cock, Paka stepped into a canoe and set out for the island of Kauai. It was a long journey and he was weary when he reached the far shore.

As he beached his canoe, a young man of chiefly bearing came along the beach. "I am Kaunalewa of Waimea," he said. "May I help the stranger?"

"I am Paka of Hawaii. Can you tell me of the lovely Makolea, carried here by servants of your king?"

Kaunalewa shook his head. "I have heard nothing of such a one. But you are weary. Come bathe, eat, and spend the night in my home. In the morning I shall make inquiries."

Gratefully Paka accepted. In the morning he woke refreshed.

"Today the king holds a boxing match," his host told him.

"Everyone will be there. Let us join the crowd and see what we can learn."

Paka nodded. "Who is champion boxer of your island?" he asked as they made their way to the sports arena.

"The king himself," Kaunalewa answered. "None can stand up to him, none knock him down."

Mingling with the crowd, Paka saw one after another of the island's fine young men go down to defeat after facing the king.

Suddenly the king caught sight of Paka and called out, "Say, stranger! Come this way and join in the games with this son of the soil!"

Paka went boldly to meet the king. "I know a little of this sport of boxing," he said, "but none have ever called me expert."

"No matter," said the king and struck Paka such a blow that he staggered and nearly fell to the ground. Recovering his balance and shaking his head to clear away the dizziness, Paka struck back. Down went the king with a thud.

When he finally got to his feet he exclaimed, "Say! That was great fun! Not one of my men has ever been able to throw me down and here you, a stranger, have done it. I have found a worthy opponent at last! Let us try a little wrestling."

So Paka took on the king in a wrestling match and to the surprise of all, broke his opponent's arm. This time, the king found it hard to hide his fury but he bared his teeth in a grin of sorts and said, "Soon we must have another contest. You will hear from me."

Paka accepted Kaunalewa's invitation to spend another night. When they reached home, he asked eagerly if his host had heard any word of Makolea.

Kaunalewa shook his head, puzzled. "If the king has brought her here, it is a well-kept secret. I have heard not a word of it, even from those who spend their time gossiping. Perhaps you are mistaken."

Next day, Paka heard the king's crier making his rounds. He felt a chill of dread as he made out the words.

"All are commanded to appear this day at the king's riddling house for the king's riddling contest with Paka of Hawaii. No man, woman, or child may remain at home except those who do not blink when a finger is poked at their eyes."

Paka said, "Call this crier here. I would speak with him."

"You cannot do that," Kaunalewa objected. "He is called The Filthy One. He performs the lowest tasks in the king's household, dresses in rags, eats only the scraps from the king's table. No one has anything to do with him."

"No matter. I would speak with him. Come!" Paka commanded. "Here is water for bathing, fresh clothing to put on, good food to eat. When you have finished, I would talk with you."

Unbelieving, the king's crier bathed, dressed himself, bolted a hasty meal, then approached uncertainly and knelt at Paka's feet.

"What do you want of me, honored stranger?"

"News," said Paka. "You are of the king's household. Is it true that he has brought the fair Makolea here from Oahu?"

The crier hesitated, trembling, then answered faintly, "It means my death if the king hears I told you, yet you are the first who has ever shown me kindness. It is true. The king's men brought Makolea here. She is kept hidden in a grass house guarded by Ebb Tide and Flow Tide. None may approach."

Paka's eyes lighted at the news. "I will find her and take her back with me!"

Kaunalewa broke in. "Paka, does this woman mean so much to you that you would defy the king?"

"Makolea is my wife," Paka answered.

Kaunalewa shook his head grimly. "This could mean your death."

"Or his," said Paka.

Kaunalewa saw it was useless to argue. "The king has challenged you to a riddling contest. Do you know anything of riddling?"

"Nothing," Paka replied. "I have had no time for such things. But I shall find a way to outwit him."

Kaunalewa accompanied Paka to the riddling house and wished him well as the crowds looked on with pity.

When the king saw him he called out, "Ho, Paka! You have bested me at boxing and wrestling. Have you courage to face me at riddling? If you lose you will bake in this oven!"

Paka answered cooly, "I will take my chances with the son of the soil. If I lose, I bake in the oven. If I win . . . you bake. Agreed?"

A gasp went up from the crowd and all eyes were on the king. He had turned pale but he could not refuse the challenge. "Agreed," he said curtly.

Paka said a silent prayer to his gods as he went forward. Beside the riddling house the imu steamed and he remembered the words of his uncle, "I see the King of Kauai standing between a grass house and a steaming oven . . . and death stands at his side." In the distance he saw another grass house with two men standing guard before it. This must be the house where Makolea was held prisoner. His mind filled with thoughts of her and he barely heard the words the king spoke:

"The riddle has two parts. Here is the first part:

The men that stand,
The men that lie down,
The men that are folded."

Paka tried to concentrate but his thoughts kept straying to the grass house with the two men standing before it.

"Come!" said the king impatiently, "did you hear?" He repeated the lines.

Paka heard the words, "The men that stand," and a wild thought flashed through his mind. Could that be the answer? There was but one way to find out.

He spoke out boldly. "The answer is a house. The men that stand are the corner posts. The men that lie down are the cross beams. The men that are folded are the bundles of thatch."

The king's face grew dark. "The stranger has a sharp wit," he said. "Is it sharp enough to answer the second part?

> Plaited at the sides,
> Plaited at the back,
> Plaited at the front,
> But leaving an opening."

Paka drew in a deep breath. What good to answer the first half correctly if he failed the second half? The wrong answer now and he would die in that steaming oven and his beloved Makolea would become the wife of this arrogant king. He tried to repeat the words of the second half of the riddle but his mind was suddenly blank.

A movement from the house in the distance caught his eye. The guards still stood watch but now in the opening stood a figure . . . the figure of Makolea!

The king, waiting, licked his lips. "Has the stranger's wit deserted him?" he taunted.

"Not so," Paka answered. "The answer to the second part is also a house, plaited with grass at sides, back, and front, with an opening —the door."

The king gave a cry of rage. It was drowned out by the shouts of his people as they moved in to form a grim circle around him. There was no escape. He was seized and thrown into the oven he had prepared for Paka.

But Paka did not stay to see. He was running to rescue Makolea.

Next morning, crowds lined the shore to see the procession that made its way to the launching place where the royal canoe waited. An attendant ran before it, calling out, "Make way! Make way for the royal party!"

First came the bearer of the king's kapu stick—the former king's crier, a man transformed. Behind him walked Paka with Makolea at his side. A young man of chiefly bearing followed.

At the water's edge, Paka turned and spoke. "People of Kauai, I thank you for your kindness to me and to my wife. May your lands increase under your new ruler . . . King Kaunalewa!"

Smiling, Kaunalewa acknowledged the cheers of his people. Paka and Makolea took their places on the pola of the royal canoe.

Paddlers bent to their paddles and they were on their way. First to Oahu for a visit with Kii-who-goes and Kii-who-stays. Then on to Hawaii. For Paka was returning home with his beloved Makolea—his chiefess won by a riddle.

Maui-the-trickster

Young Maui came of a proud family line, carried on in the names of its sons. But never had the family known such a son as this youngest. He had magic powers, he had performed heroic deeds— and he was a mischievous trickster. . . .

IT WAS THE night before the lifting of the kapu on aku fishing, and Maui's brothers were planning the next day's expedition.

Maui-first-born said, "Tomorrow I shall be fisherman. You, Maui-second-born shall be steersman. You, Maui-third-born, paddler."

"And what of me?" asked young Maui.

"You are no fisherman," said his brother. "You have no place in our canoe."

66

Young Maui gave him a sly look but said no more.

Before daybreak, the three brothers were on their way to the fishing koa. Young Maui stood on shore watching as their canoe moved steadily out toward deep water.

Maui-first-born gave directions to the steersman. "See that flock of low-flying birds? Follow it. That is where the aku feed today."

They reached the spot and dropped their lines, waiting patiently. No luck. Maui-first-born, pulling up his line, stopped to watch the strange behavior of a seabird. It circled their canoe, flew a little way, then waited.

"Follow that bird!" he ordered.

The canoe followed, stopping where the bird stopped, and Maui-first-born let down his hook. At once he felt the line throb. He pulled. Up came a fine fat aku.

But before he could bring it into the canoe, the seabird swooped down with a shrill cry and snatched it from his hook. Perching brazenly on the prow of the canoe, it proceeded to eat the fish.

Angrily, Maui-first-born struck out with his paddle. The seabird vanished and in its place sat Maui-the-trickster, sucking noisily on a fishbone.

"What luck, my brothers?" he asked with a mischievous grin.

"You should know, you thieving rascal!" cried his oldest brother.

Maui's laughter turned to a shrill squawk. He resumed his seabird form and flew off shoreward.

The following day, Maui-second-born was fisherman. All three brothers kept a sharp lookout for the rascal seabird but saw no sign of it.

When the sun was high overhead, the brothers were still without a catch. Maui-second-born growled, "The fish do not like this turtle-shell hook. Open my calabash and get out my bone hook."

His brother lifted the lid of the calabash. Out fluttered a white cock. Perching on the prow, it flapped its wings and crowed, loud and long.

Maui-second-born threw down his line in disgust. "No use to fish any longer! That noise has scared off every fish within miles! How did a cock get into my fishing calabash?"

"Just a bit of magic," said a familiar voice and there in place of the white cock stood Maui-the-trickster, flapping his arms and crowing.

Next day it was Maui-third-born's turn as fisherman. Before they left shore he searched canoe and calabash carefully.

Out at the place where the fish gathered, he baited his favorite shell hook and dropped his line. For nearly an hour he sat waiting. Then, a tug. "I have one!" he cried. "Keep watch for that trickster!"

There was no sign of crowing cock or wheeling seabird. But just as the fish cleared the water, a small merry voice chirped, "Watch out! Keep your line taut or you will lose him!"

Startled, Maui-third-born turned. With a splash his fish was gone. Crawling up from the floor of the canoe came a lively brown cockroach, and there, once again, was Maui-the-trickster.

"Throw the trouble-maker overboard! Let him swim ashore!" cried Maui-first-born.

The three reached for Maui and pushed him into the water, only to see him take on his seabird form and fly away with a taunting cry.

Four days went by and the Maui brothers brought in not a single fish. Their angry wives scolded, their hungry children cried, their luckier neighbors avoided them.

Young Maui said, "If you would but take me as fisherman today, your luck would change. I have a magic fish hook that would bring in such a fish as none have ever seen."

"You would find fish where skilled fishermen have failed?" Maui-third-born demanded.

"I would," said Maui. "I tell you, this is a rare hook indeed. There has never been one like it."

"Oh, let him come," said Maui-second-born wearily. "When Maui-the-boaster finds out there is more to fishing than idle talk, he will be glad to leave us alone."

Scowling, the brothers took their places as steersman and paddlers. Maui placed a great coil of olona cord on the floor of the canoe and tucked his special fish hook into the waistband of his malo, then took his place.

"Steer for deep water!" he ordered. The brothers paddled out in silence.

When they reached their favorite spot, Maui-second-born said, "This is where the fish stay."

"Ae. But who wants a place where they stay?" Maui asked. "I seek a place they are eager to leave! Paddle on!"

The canoe went out a long way, then the eldest brother said, "Surely this is far enough out, even for you Maui."

"For me, perhaps, but not for the giant fish I plan to catch. He lives in deeper water still. Paddle on. I will tell you when to stop," said Maui.

Grimly the brothers paddled on until their island lay far behind them and nothing but open sea met their eyes.

"Here!" said Maui at last.

The paddlers held the canoe in place and watched skeptically as Maui uncoiled his long line of olona fiber and fastened on his strong barbed hook. He baited it and dropped it over the side.

Down . . . down . . . down . . . down went the magic hook. The brothers smiled as Maui continued to pay out his line with no sign of a strike. Then, all at once, the line grew taut. Maui leaned back, testing it.

"I have him!" he cried. "Too large to bring into the canoe, this one. Paddle for shore! I'll tow him behind. Make haste!"

The brothers bent to their paddles, dipping and pulling, dipping and pulling, yet the canoe seemed almost to stand still. Maui-first-born turned to look back.

"Keep going!" Maui shouted. "Don't look back! Do you want to lose our prize catch?"

The brothers paddled harder, but a thoughtful frown grew on the face of Maui-first-born. What kind of fish was this on Maui's line? A tremendous one, no doubt of that. But there was something strange about it. No leaping and struggling to get free . . . no slackening and tightening of the line . . . no shuddering and lurching of the canoe. Only a dead weight dragging behind. Suspicious, he turned and looked back.

He gave a cry of terror. Rising out of the sea came the menacing head of a great black island, bearing down on them like a giant fish. Stunned, Maui-first-born dropped his paddle. The others whirled about.

The spell was broken. With a loud crack, the island tore loose and slid back into the sea.

"O my brothers!" cried Maui. "You had a fish such as none have ever seen! You could have been the most famous fishermen in the islands! Auwe! What a pity you looked back and lost it!"

The Riddling Chief of Puna

Riddling was a chiefly skill, for few but chiefs had time for such long and difficult training. Did a chief lack patience for such training? There were other ways of gaining a reputation as a riddler—and no way more cruel than that used by the Riddling Chief of Puna. . . .

THERE ONCE LIVED a man of royal blood who was known as the Riddling Chief of Puna. He had but one ambition—to build the greatest collection of riddles ever known.

From time to time he would send a young man out in search of additions. If he found one, the chief, unwilling to have the answer known even by its finder, would turn on him with his own terrible riddle and say,

72

"Mo-ke-ki a mo-ke-ki!
Answer *my* riddle or die in the oven!"

Since no man living knew what that riddle asked, how could he answer? One after another, youths met death in the chief's imu until Puna was in danger of becoming a district of old men.

Among the few remaining youths was one called Hoopai, joy of his parents' life. He was their one surviving son, his elder brother having died in the chief's oven just six months earlier when he failed to answer the dreadful riddle.

Great was the sorrow of Hoopai's parents when they heard that he too had been ordered to find a new riddle for the chief. "Now we shall be left childless," they mourned, "for even though you find the rarest riddle known, you will die as your brother did, unless you find an answer to the chief's own death-dealing riddle, as well."

"Then I must find that answer," said Hoopai, and he set out to do so. In every corner of the district, Hoopai asked but many had lost sons to the cruel chief and few would tell what riddles they knew.

On around the island he went, through the districts of Kau and Kona, through Kohala and Hamakua, through Hilo and back to Puna. In his journey he found three riddles but no answer at all to the chief's death-dealing riddle. The future for Hoopai looked gloomy indeed.

As he made his way through the village of Olaa, he saw an elderly couple slowly and painfully cultivating their small plot of land.

"Here, let me do that, Kupuna," said Hoopai, taking the digging stick from the old man's hand. "You have reached an age when you should be taking your rest."

"Auwe! For us there will be no rest!" the old woman mourned.

"First our son, then our grandson, was thrown into the chief's oven because he could not answer the chief's imu-feeding riddle."

"Alas, I may soon follow them," said Hoopai, "for it is on this same errand I have come."

The old man shook his head sorrowfully. "Ah, if we could but help you! To save your life would avenge the death of our son and grandson. What is the riddle the chief asks?"

"It is but a line. One line, then death," Hoopai answered. "Mo-ke-ki a mo-ke-ki."

The old man rubbed his forehead. "If my memory were but stronger," he lamented. "As a young man I was an attendant of this chief's father. There was a riddle told at court in those times, but auwe! It has slipped from my brain like water from a sieve! It had something to do with the parts of the body, but what? I can no longer say. But come in and eat with us and spend the night."

In the morning, Hoopai thanked the old couple and continued on his way. As he walked, he turned over in his mind what the old man had said. Something to do with parts of the body. . . . Mo-ke-ki. . . . Could it be that the answer was a part of the body whose name contained the syllable *ki?* He ran over some of those words. There was ki-no, the body . . . ki-hi-poo, the head. There were other such words. He racked his brain to think of them. Could the answer lie in this direction? He would have to risk it. He had found nothing better.

So Hoopai reported back to the chief, who greeted him with a crafty smile. "You must be weary, Hoopai," he said. "Go home and take your rest. In the morning come and tell me what you have found."

As soon as Hoopai left, the chief gave orders to his servants to prepare the imu that was dug beside the chief's house. Two men laid the kindling and firewood. Two lighted the fire. Two placed a

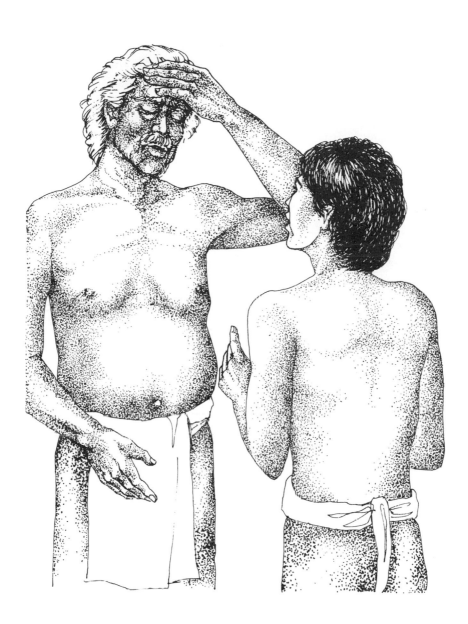

layer of stones. Two covered it with layers of grass, ti leaves, and matting.

All night the imu burned. In the morning Hoopai was brought before the chief, who stood between his royal house and the earth oven. At a signal, guards moved up to form a square forty yards long and forty yards wide so that no one might come close enough to hear the riddles.

The chief nodded and Hoopai spoke.

> "O Chief of Puna,
> O Collector of Riddles,
> I have brought you a treasure,
> A treasure for your collection."

"Good," said the chief. "Let me hear it."

Hoopai said,

> "I have a house—
> A house with eight rafters,
> A house with one post.
> I carry it with me.
> It gives me shelter."

The chief frowned. "A house that you carry with you? What could this be?"

"An umbrella, my chief," Hoopai answered.

"Clever," said the chief. "Very clever indeed." He motioned. Two guards approached, removed the layer of mats from the imu and returned to their places. The chief said to Hoopai, "Would you, by chance, have a second riddle?"

"By chance, I would," Hoopai answered.

> "My old man—
> He cries day and night,

Through rain and sunshine,
Through wet season and dry.
Listen! You can hear him now."

So well did Hoopai deliver his lines that the chief unconsciously put his hand to his ear to listen, and heard in the distance the rise and fall of the sea on the shore, a sound that went on without ending.

"The surf!" cried the king. "Wise! Very wise indeed!" He motioned again. Two guards approached, removed the layer of ti leaves from the imu and returned to their places. The chief said to Hoopai, "You would not, by chance, have a third riddle for me?"

"By chance, I would," Hoopai answered.

"My twin—
With me from the day I crawled,
With me till the day I die.
I cannot escape him,
Yet when storms come,
He deserts me."

The chief puzzled over this one and had to ask the answer. Hoopai gave it—"my shadow."

"Droll," said the chief. "Very droll indeed." He motioned once more. Two guards approached, removed the layer of grass from the imu and returned to their places. Steam rose up in a cloud and Hoopai knew that death was very near.

"Would you, by chance, have any more riddles for me?" the chief asked.

"Auwe! No more," said Hoopai.

The chief's eyes gleamed. "Then I have one for you!" he cried.

> "Mo-ke-ki a mo-ke-ki!
> Give me the answer
> Or die in the oven!"

Hoopai answered bravely,

> "Mo-ke-ki a mo-kc-ki!
> I have an answer to Mo-ke-ki!"

The chief looked stunned at his unexpected reply. Recovering, he blustered, "I do not believe you! If you truly have the answer I shall bake in my own oven. If you have not, you shall bake!

> Mo-ke-ki a mo-ke-ki!
> Where did you find the answer
> To Mo-ke-ki?"

Hoopai said a silent prayer to his gods, then spoke:

> "Ki-hi-po a ki-hi-po!
> I found the answer in my head:
> Ki-hi-po!
> The riddle now is answered.
> Time to feed the imu!
> Its food? Your body! Ki-no!"

The chief looked about in terror for a way to escape. In a voice that carried clearly to the waiting guards, Hoopai declared, "By his own conditions, the chief has forfeited his life!"

Those were the terms. The men were happy to carry them out. Scarcely one of them had not lost a son or brother to this cruel chief. Grimly they closed in, picked him up, and tossed him into his own imu.

That was the end of the Riddling Chief of Puna. But to this day, it is very difficult to find anyone in the district of Puna who will tell you a riddle. When you ask, they shake their heads and say, "No riddles. It was for this that the bones of our ancestors baked in the imu."

Iwa the Crafty One

To a grasping chief, a rascal might prove more useful than an honest man. What greater rascal could be found than Iwa the Crafty One? It was said that he could pluck the teeth from a warrior's jawbone and the warrior never miss them until his next meal. . . .

THE HIGH CHIEF was enjoying his favorite pastime, squid fishing. But something had gone wrong. Iwa and his friend Hoapili, watching from the beach, saw one after another of the chief's men dive from the pola of the royal canoe, and surface again, empty-handed.

"What do they seek?" Hoapili asked.

Iwa shrugged. "Who knows?"

Soon, one of the chief's men swam ashore with a message.

"What is it you dive for?" asked Hoapili.

"The chief's fire shell—his favorite red cowrey that brought the squid swarming to his line. This morning it must have become wedged in the deepest coral. None have been able to dive deep enough to find it. Who is champion diver of the district?"

Hoapili laughed. "Iwa here is the one to help you. He can walk on the ocean's floor, this one!"

"Then come," said the messenger. He plunged back into the water and Iwa followed. When they reached the royal canoe he said, "O my chief, this is Iwa, champion diver of the district."

"You, Iwa!" said the High Chief. "Can you dive down and recover my shell of fire?"

"Auwe, O Chief, I cannot."

"How is this?"

"The shell is not there," Iwa replied softly.

"How could you know this?" demanded the High Chief.

"It was I who removed it before daybreak and tied your line to the coral," came the cool reply.

The chief's face grew dark. "You will never die of old age, Brazen One, stealing royal property! When tomorrow's sun rises, have my fire shell here or I shall use your head for fish bait!"

When the morrow's sun rose red in the sky, Iwa returned with the fire shell.

"Your head, for the moment, is safe," said the High Chief. He studied Iwa thoughtfully. "Since you are so fond of stealing royal property I will give you an opportunity. In the valley of Waipio stands the sacred temple of Pakaalana. Within it, closely guarded, hangs my sacred stone axe. Bring it to me and you live. Fail and you die by that axe."

Iwa soon learned that the sacred axe hung from a rope whose

ends were tied about the necks of two old women charged with its safety. The entire valley in which the temple stood, was under strict kapu. Each evening at dusk, the High Chief's crier, carrying his tapa flag, would run from the nearest to the farthest boundary, crying:

> "Sleep—for the sacred axe of the High Chief
>   is kapu.
> Kapu—let no man go forth from his house.
> Kapu—let no dog bark.
> Kapu—let no pig squeal.
> Kapu—let no rooster crow.
> Sleep, sleep—until the kapu is raised."

Iwa gave the matter careful thought, then made his plan. He visited the crier and said, "The High Chief has need of you at the seashore. I am to take your place this night in the valley."

The crier, used to the High Chief's whims, hurried off toward the seashore. Just before dusk, Iwa began the circuit of the valley, carrying the crier's tapa flag and sounding the crier's warning. Everyone hurried into his house and remained there.

When Iwa reached the temple of Pakaalana he called out, "Where are the guardians of the High Chief's kapu axe? Are they sleeping?"

"No indeed. We are awake," the guardians answered, "and the kapu axe is safe."

"Let me feel the axe to make sure it is safe," said Iwa. He reached out, wrenched the axe free, and pulling on the rope, sent the two guardians crashing into each other.

"Thief! Thief!" they cried. "A thief steals the High Chief's kapu axe!"

But the people of the valley, fearful of the kapu, were slow to

respond. Iwa had reached the foot of the trail before the first man ventured out of his house. He was halfway to the top of the trail before the others reached the foot. Knowing they could not overtake him, the men returned to their houses.

Next morning when the High Chief saw Iwa in the crowd assembled before his residence, he laughed. "So, Clever One! You have given up, have you? I thought you would not be able to get the kapu axe."

Iwa came forward. "I brought this axe, O Chief," he said. "Perhaps it is the wrong one."

The High Chief took the axe and recognized it as his own. "You are a clever thief indeed," he said. "You could be a useful member of my court. I would test you further. Would you stake your bones on your skill?"

"Ae, O Chief, I would," Iwa replied.

The eyes of the High Chief gleamed. "Then here is my thought for you. You shall match wits with the six cleverest thieves in my chiefdom. Two houses will be set aside—one for you, one for them —to be filled with all manner of things that can be taken in one night. Win, and you live. Lose, and you die. Agreed?"

"Agreed, O Chief," said Iwa. "To compete against seven might be difficult. But six? No problem."

The High Chief summoned his six thieves, one from each district of the island. From Kohala and Hamakua, from Hilo and Puna, from Kau and Kona they came.

At dusk, the contest began. The six thieves set to work at once, stealing everything they could lay hands on, and storing it in their house. But Iwa, yawning, went into his house, lay down, and went to sleep.

All night the thieves worked. A little before dawn, no room was left in their house for another thing so they lay down outside and went to sleep.

When the first cock crowed, Iwa woke, stretched, and said, "Time to get to work." Moving quietly past the sleeping thieves, he skillfully moved everything from their house into his own. Then he made a brief visit to the High Chief's royal sleeping house, added one item to his collection, and lay down to sleep.

Soon after daylight, the High Chief woke shivering, to find that his royal sleeping kapa had slipped off during the night. Dressing quickly, he hurried out to see how the contest had ended.

At the first house the six thieves still slumbered outside. The High Chief peered inside. Empty.

He moved to Iwa's house. Iwa too, was sleeping, undisturbed by the cackling of a plump hen, the howling of a thin dog, the squealing of a fat pig, all tied to the doorpost. There was no need to look inside. Iwa's collection came tumbling out the door to meet him.

Breadfruit, taro root, and sweet potatoes . . . water gourds, poi pounders, and calabashes . . . eel traps, fishing nets, and canoe paddles. Hardly an item of daily use in the village was not represented in Iwa's collection. Digging sticks, tapa beaters, carrying poles, and sling nets . . . shell trumpets, nose flutes, bamboo rattles, and coconut drums . . . short spears, long spears, wooden daggers, and shark-tooth clubs . . . and on top of the pile—the High Chief's royal sleeping kapa.

When he saw this, the chief roared with laughter—laughter that saved Iwa's life and won for him a place guarding the High Chief's treasures. And you may be sure that nothing was stolen from the royal storehouse while Iwa the Crafty One was there to guard it!

The Riddling Youngster

In Old Hawaii a man born a commoner found few opportunities to improve his lot. But an expert riddler, whether chief or commoner, could win fame and fortune. Had he a quick wit? Could he match word for word, idea for idea, insult for insult, action for action? Express himself in chant form on any subject? Such a one might become champion riddler and win a position of respect—or lose his bones. . . .

IT WAS RIDDLING time for Halepaki and his son, Kai-palaoa. Each morning they spent long hours together in the giving and answering of riddles, in the creating of chants, in the matching of wits.

Halepaki had scarcely seated himself when his son began. "I have a fine riddle for you this morning, my father! Listen!

> The back is thin,
> The front is thin,
> The bones outside,
> The skin inside,
> It flies but cannot walk."

Halepaki buried his face in his hands. "A strange animal, this one, with bones on the outside and skin on the inside," he murmured.

"You can't guess it! I've caught you at last!" Kai cried.

His father raised his head. "I wonder . . ." he began slowly, "could it be . . . a kite?"

Kai's face fell. "How did you guess it?"

Halepaki's eyes twinkled. "This riddle—it is one you learned from your mother, eh?"

Kai nodded. "How could you know that?"

"Because it is one she learned from me."

Father and son broke into laughter. Kai said, "Here is another. This one you have not heard. I made it up myself:

> Green as grass,
> White as snow,
> Red as fire,
> Black as lava,
> It tastes good to the tongue."

Halepaki repeated the words softly to himself, was silent for a moment, then asked, "Could it be the watermelon?"

"Ae, watermelon!" Kai shouted. "Your favorite fruit!"

"So it is." Halepaki chuckled. "Now let me ask you one, my sharp-witted son.

Useful to man,
Though full of holes;
The more holes you add,
The more it can carry."

Kai frowned. "Useful yet full of holes! A sieve? But a sieve carries nothing!"

"True. But you swim in the right direction, Clever One."

Kai whispered the last line again. "The more holes you add, the more it can carry . . . I have it! A fishnet!"

"Aia la! You will be a better riddler than your father, before long!" Halepaki cried.

"Not so," Kai protested. "You are the finest riddler in the islands!"

"Ah, no," Halepaki answered. "Kalani, High Chief of Kauai, is counted champion. But someday when I have learned enough, I shall challenge the great Kalani."

"And then you will be champion riddler of the islands," Kai said confidently.

"And you, the riddling youngster," said Halepaki.

The day soon came when Halepaki set out to challenge the champion. Kai and his mother stood on the beach watching his father's canoe make its way past Mokuola, the tiny islet in the bay, then head out into deep water toward the island of Kauai in the western sea.

The new moon grew to roundness and moved on to smallness, once . . . twice . . . three times . . . and four, and no word came from Halepaki.

Kai and his mother stared out to sea, straining for a glimpse of Halepaki's canoe beyond the waving coco palms of Mokuola. Island of Refuge, it was called, and there, one in trouble could flee from any island, for refuge. But for Kai and his mother there was no refuge from anxiety.

"Some evil has surely befallen your father or he would have sent word before this," Kai's mother said sorrowfully.

"I will go in search of him," said Kai. "But before I set foot on the island of the riddling champion I must learn all that I can of my father's art. Will you teach me what you know of riddling, my mother?"

Kai learned all that his mother could teach him, of the things above and the things below, of life in the uplands and life in the lowlands, of distant places on his island and their special characteristics. Then she said, "Now you must go to your aunt in Kohala. She married my brother who was a fine riddler, and she has lived on the island of Kauai and can teach you much that I do not know."

So Kai journeyed to Kohala and learned from his aunt all that she could teach him, of things that happen by day and things that happen by night, of good and of evil, of life and of death, of distant places on the island of Kauai and their special characteristics. When she had taught him all she knew, he was classed as an expert although he was still a youngster.

Then Kai carefully chose the largest calabash he could find, and packed it with a variety of articles that might be helpful to him in his mission. He bade farewell to his aunt and mother, stepped into his canoe, and went in search of his father.

When he reached the island of Kauai, a fleet of fishing canoes was unloading its catch. Standing on the beach, watching, was a handsome youth about his own age. Kai approached him and said, "I am Kai-palaoa of Hawaii. Can you give me news of Halepaki the riddler who came to challenge your High Chief four moons ago?"

The youth gave him a strange look and pointed. "The flag of the

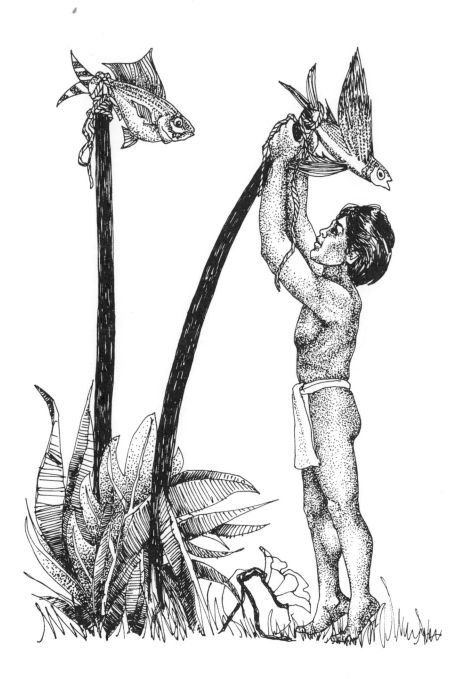

High Chief still flies; his kapu stick still stands," he said. "Halepaki challenged and lost. His bones lie bleaching in the High Chief's House-of-Bones, his teeth in his Fence-of-Teeth."

Kai's heart grew heavy at the news.

"What was this man Halepaki to you?" the youth asked.

"He was my father." Kai thought he saw a look of compassion cross the stranger's face but it was gone in a flash and the youth said nothing more. Kai drew a deep breath. He knew now that he must challenge the High Chief of Kauai; avenge his father . . . or join him.

He turned and went to the head fisherman. "I am a stranger who has come on a long journey," he said. "Can you spare me a few fish?"

"Take what you need," said the man.

Kai studied the catch carefully, then chose two fish. The first was black with a reddish-yellow top fin that gave it the name "waving flag." The second was one whose name meant "brave challenge."

"You take but two," the fisherman commented. "You have a small hunger."

"Not so," Kai replied. "My hunger is great, but for revenge, not food. Tell me, who is that youth?"

"He is Kelii—Young Chief, younger brother of Kalani the High Chief."

Kai turned for another look but Kelii had disappeared. Kai strode to the chief's flagstaff, tore down the chief's flag and hung in its place his fish called "waving flag." He snatched the white kapa ball from the chief's kapu stick and replaced it with his fish, "brave challenge."

Soon a messenger appeared in answer to this defiance. He called down, "The High Chief orders you to come up, young braggart!"

Kai replied, "The stranger orders you to come down, middle-aged braggart!"

Amused at his impudence, the chief's messenger came down and escorted Kai, with his riddler's calabash, to the High Chief. At the door of the riddling house he was challenged by Keeper of the Bones.

"Who are you and what do you seek?"

"I am Kai-palaoa, son of Halepaki the riddler, of Hawaii. I come to challenge your chief to a contest of wits."

"Ho! Listen to the riddling youngster!" jeered Keeper of the Bones. "If it is a contest you want, a contest you shall have. But you are too young to enter the riddling house. You shall remain outside. Outside you shall compete, outside eat and sleep, and outside die."

"If I am too young to enter the riddling house, your chief is too old to leave it. He shall remain inside. Inside he shall compete, inside eat and sleep, and inside die."

At this, the angry voice of the High Chief was heard from inside. "Enough! Am I to spend the time of the contest shut up in here while this youngster is free to come and go? The young braggart has outwitted you! Bid him enter."

Scowling, Keeper of the Bones moved aside and Kai entered. He saw the High Chief seated on a platform covered with fine woven matting. Behind him stood six warriors. On his left stood Keeper of the Teeth.

Keeper of the Bones, instead of taking his place on the chief's right, proceeded to tear up the matting from one half of the floor. Then he spilled out the contents of a water gourd, turning the earthen floor to mud. Taking his place on the matting-covered platform he said with a look of malice, "We regret that we have no fine mat like the chief's, to offer the stranger."

Kai calmly opened his calabash, took out handfuls of grass and threw them down upon the muddy floor. He covered the grass, first with a coarse kapa, then with a finely-made, sweetly-scented kapa, and answered, "I regret that I have no fine kapa like mine, to offer the chief."

The High Chief's face grew dark. "You would challenge me to a contest of wits, knowing that your father's skill was not enough to save him?" he demanded.

"I would," Kai replied.

"For what stakes?

"My bones against your bones."

The High Chief looked startled. Keeper of the Bones said with an evil grin, "O Chief, your House-of-Bones and Fence-of-Teeth lack but one set each. This one's bones are young and soft, his teeth short and white, but they will do."

Kai grinned. "The chief's bones are old and brittle, his teeth long and yellow, but they will do."

The High Chief gave an angry bellow. "Begin the contest!"

Keeper of Teeth said to Kai, "As challenger, you have the choice of referee. My services are available."

"Mahalo," said Kai curtly. "I have another choice."

The chief and his two attendants studied him uneasily. "Who is your choice?" Keeper of Teeth demanded.

"Kelii," Kai answered.

The three looked amused. Kai felt a chill of dread. Had he mistaken the look of sympathy in Kelii's face? Even so, Kai felt him to be a better choice than Keeper of Teeth.

Kelii was summoned. He looked straight at Kai as he entered but his face remained expressionless. The three showed no doubt of Kelii's support as he took his place upon the platform.

Keeper of Bones said smoothly, "Before such an important event, it is fitting that we drink of ceremonial awa and eat of baked pig."

He turned to Keeper of Teeth. "Check the imu. See if our pig is ready while I prepare the awa root."

Keeper of Teeth went out. Soon Kai smelled the appetizing aroma of roasting pork. Calmly he reached into his calabash and chose what he needed: pebbles, kindling, fire sticks, and a small wooden pig wound about with string. He dug a small hole in the earthen floor, built a small imu, lighted a small fire. Then, taking up his small wooden pig, he pulled the string. It unwound with a squealing sound.

"Such a noisy one, this pig!" Kai exclaimed. He went through the motions of killing and cleaning it. In the hollow center he tucked a portion of baked pork he had brought with him. Then he placed his miniature pig in his miniature imu, covered it with pebbles, grass, and damp kapa mats, and sat back on his heels with a sigh of satisfaction.

"Now while my pig bakes, I shall prepare my awa," he said. From the calabash came pieces of awa root already pounded, and his stone pounder. He gave the roots a few token strokes, placed them in a piece of palm fiber and adding water, strained the liquid into his drinking bowl.

While Keeper of Bones was still pounding awa root for the High Chief's ceremonial drink, Kai was already making his offering to his gods and drinking his. While Keeper of Teeth was still watching the chief's imu, Kai was taking his miniature pig from his miniature imu, removing the portion of baked pork, and eating with good appetite.

But when the royal meal was ready, the High Chief took little pleasure in it, for Kai, who should have been watching, hungry and envious, was instead finishing his own tasty meal.

"Clear this away!" the chief ordered. "Let the contest begin!"

Kelii came forward and announced in a cold voice, "A contest of wits between Kalani, High Chief of the island of Kauai, and Kai-palaoa, riddling youngster from the island of Hawaii. Five rounds to be played. If tied score, another contest tomorrow. The stakes, their bones. Winner to go free, loser to be baked in the imu. First, let each compose a chant telling of the wonders to be found only on his own island. The High Chief goes first."

The High Chief thought for a moment, then began his chant:

> "How beautiful is the island of Kauai!
> Island of the barking sand,
> Island of the spouting horn,
> Island of the great canyon
> And the mountain of rippling waters."

Kai nodded his appreciation and responded:

> "How beautiful is Hawaii!
> Island of the black sand,
> Island of the white mountain,
> Island of the five volcanoes
> And the home of eternal fire."

Kelii announced a tie. "First round . . . pai a pai. Now let us have a round of match and top."

The High Chief looked smug and began at once: "I speak of an animal of great wisdom. The yellow-backed crab is small and must go crawling. But he carries his bones on the outside to protect the meat inside. His legs are ten."

Kai retorted, "I speak of an animal of great wisdom. The red rock lobster is small and must go crawling. But he carries his bones on the outside to protect the meat inside. His legs are fourteen."

"Second round . . . pai a pai," Kelii droned. "Now let us hear of foods that grow below ground."

To himself, the High Chief counted some off on his fingers, then began:

> "Below the ground,
> Below the ground,
> These do grow below the ground:
> The root of the potato,
> The root of the sweet potato,
> The root of the yam,
> And the arrowroot."

Kai responded promptly:

> "Below the ground,
> Below the ground,
> These do grow below the ground:
> The root of sweet fern,
> The root of wetland taro,
> The root of dryland taro,
> And the awa root
> Which makes man forget all others."

"Third round . . . pai a pai," said Kelii. "Now of foods that grow above ground."

High Chief was full of assurance. He began at once:

> "Above the ground,
> Above the ground,
> These do grow above the ground:
> Fruit of the banana,
> Fruit of the mountain apple,
> Fruit of the sugar cane,
> And the breadfruit."

Kai's answer came swiftly:

> "Above the ground,
> Above the ground,
> These do grow above the ground:
> Fruit of the palm—the coconut,
> Fruit of the bird—the egg,
> Fruit of the night—the moon,
> Fruit of the day—the sun,
> Which nourishes all other fruits."

There was no doubt about that round. Kai's last line had certainly matched and topped the High Chief's. "Fourth round . . . still a tie. One round to go," Kelii declared. "Let us hear now of canoe travels."

High Chief thought for a moment, then a sly grin spread across his face. Arrogantly he began his chant:

> "My canoe sails to the islands:
> To Niihau, to Kauai,
> To Oahu and Molokai,
> To Lanai and Kahoolawe,
> To Maui and Hawaii,
> And then turns home—
> For there are no more islands."

This time, Kai seemed to have no ready answer. He sat, head in hands, lost in thought. High Chief nodded triumphantly. Keeper of Bones rubbed his hands, as if already preparing Kai's bones for the chief's monstrous house. Keeper of Teeth licked his lips expectantly. Kelii's face remained expressionless.

High Chief began a mocking chant:

"The answer is yet to come.
It is for you to answer;
It is for us to listen.
We wait, but hear nothing."

Slowly Kai raised his head and began repeating the words of the chief's earlier chant. The riddling house grew still as death.

"My canoe sails to the islands:
To Niihau, to Kauai,
To Oahu and Molokai,
To Lanai and Kahoolawe,
To Maui and Hawaii,
And then turns home—
To Mokuola, Island of Refuge
For all the islands!"

Kai had surely topped the High Chief's chant, but his life now depended on Kelii's decision. Would Young Chief give a fair verdict, even though it meant death for his older brother? The riddling house seemed filled with flashing lightning as High Chief, Keeper of Bones, and Keeper of Teeth sent unspoken messages flying through the air to Kelii.

Young Chief's face was a carved mask. Suddenly, he pointed . . . to High Chief and his men!

A shudder ran through Kai. He had lost. His bones would now join those of his father; and his mother, waiting beyond the Island of Refuge, would never see husband or son again.

Then Kai heard Young Chief's words. "Mea i poho . . . the loser!"

Kai saw Kelii's hand rise and fall . . . not once, but three times.

He saw the warriors move in swiftly and carry out High Chief . . . Keeper of Bones . . . Keeper of Teeth, to the waiting imu.

Kai approached the platform and knelt before Young Chief. "I owe my life to you," he said.

Kelii's face lost its frozen look. He shook his head. "Your father's life I could not save," he said. "Yours I could not sacrifice. Now that I am High Chief, there will be no more riddling for such stakes on the island of Kauai. When you have taken your father's bones home for burial, the House-of-Bones and Fence-of-Teeth will be destroyed."

Then Kai-palaoa the riddling youngster who had become riddling champion, having accomplished what he had set out to do, gathered up the bones of his father for their last sad journey home.

Glossary

When the original edition of this book was published, diacritical marks in Hawaiian words were largely ignored. This attitude has changed, however, and the use of macrons and glottal stops is now encouraged by authorities in the Hawaiian language community. Although it was not possible to add diacritical marks throughout the text, the marks have been added here to show the reader the proper form of the Hawaiian words used in this book.

Originally there was no written Hawaiian language, only a spoken one. Later, when a written language was needed, it was found that all the sounds could be expressed with twelve Roman letters: five vowels and seven consonants.

The vowels each have a single sound:

a—ah e—ay i—ee o—oh u—oo

The consonants have the same sounds as they do in English. The seven consonants used are: h, k, l, m, n, p, w

Pronunciation follows two simple rules. First, every vowel is sounded: Hi'iaka is pronounced hee-ee-ah-kah. Second, every syllable ends in a vowel: Kaho'olawe is pronounced Ka-ho-o-la-ve.

The diacritical marks mentioned above help pronunciation. The macron (⁻) denotes a long stress. The glottal stop (') indicates a catch of the breath similar to that between the vowel sound *oh oh!* in English.

'ae (*a*-e), yes
'ahi (*a*-hi), deep-sea tuna, caught with very long line
aia ho'i (*ai*-a ho-i), Look! See that!
aia lā (*ai*-a *la*), There! I told you so!
aku (*a*-ku), deep-sea fish, caught with pole and line
Alaka'i (*A*-la-*ka*-i), leader; a chief of Kohala
'ama'ama (*a*-ma-*a*-ma), mullet; often kept in chief's fishpond
'ape (*a*-pe), plant with large, heart-shaped leaves
auwē (au-*we*), exclamation of dismay
'awa (*a*-va), ceremonial drink made from root of a shrub
'Ehā (E-*ha*), four
'Ekahi (E-*ka*-hi), one
'Ekolu (E-*ko*-lu), three
'Elima (E-*li*-ma), five
'Elua (E-*lu*-a), two

101

hala (*ha*-la), fruit of pūhala tree

Halepāki (*Ha*-le-*pa*-ki), father of Riddling Youngster

Hāmākua (*Ha*-ma-*ku*-a), one of six districts of island of Hawai'i

Hana hou! (*Ha*-na-*ho*-u), Do it again!

Hawai'i (Ha-*vai*-i or Ha-*wai*-i), largest island of Hawaiian chain

Hele mai e'ai (*He*-le *mai* e *ai*), Come and eat

Hilo (*Hi*-lo), district of island of Hawai'i

Hoapili (*Ho*-a-*pi*-li), friend; companion of Iwa the Crafty One

hōlua (ho-*lu*-a), Hawaiian sled used on grassy or muddy course

Ho'opa'i (*Ho*-o-*pa*-i), revenge; youth who outwitted Riddling Chief of Puna

hula (*hu*-la), traditional dance, originally sacred

'i'iwi (i-*i*-vi), scarlet and black bird whose feathers were prized for featherwork

imu (*i*-mu), earth oven; baking in imu often used in ancient times as death penalty

'Iwa (*I*-va), the Crafty One, trickster and thief

Kahiki (Ka-*hi*-ki), elder brother of Kamapua'a

kahuna (ka-*hu*-na), priest

Kaho'olawe (*Ka*-ho-o-*la*-ve), barren island within sight of Lāna'i

Kai-palaoa (*Kai*-pa-la-*o*-a), the Riddling Youngster

Kalani (Ka-*la* ni), High Chief of Kaua'i, riddling champion

kalo (*ka*-lo), taro; plant from whose roots poi is made

Kamapua'a (*Ka*-ma-pu-*a*-a), mischievous kupua, the Hog Child

kapa (*ka*-pa), tapa; cloth made from bark

kapu (*ka*-pu), forbidden

Ka'ū (Ka-*u*), dry dusty district of island of Hawai'i

Kaua'i (*Ka*-u-*a*-i), island ruled by High Chief Kalani, riddling champion

Ka-ulu-lā'au (Ka-*u*-lu-la-*au*), mischievous son of King of Maui; one who outwitted spirits of Lāna'i

Kaunalewa (*Kau*-na-*le*-va), young chief who befriended Paka

Keli'i (Ke-*li*-i), young chief; saved life of Kai, the Riddling Youngster

kī (ki), ti; plant whose leaves are used for wrapping food and covering imu

kihipo'o (*ki*-hi-*po*-o), head

Ki'i-who-goes (*Ki*-i), Paka's swift-running uncle

Ki'i-who-stays (*Ki*-i), Paka's prophesying uncle

kino (*ki*-no), body

koa (*ko*-a), hard wood

Kohala (Ko-*ha*-la), district of Hawai'i; home of Pūpū

Kona (*Ko*-na), district of Hawai'i; home of Mākolea

kukui (ku-*ku*-i), nut whose oil fishermen used to smooth the water

Kūpa'a (Ku-*pa*-a), loyal; steward of Chief Alaka'i

kupua (ku-*pu*-a), one with supernatural powers

Kupuna (Ku-*pu*-na), grandmother; grandfather

lei (*le*-i), garland of flowers or leaves

Lāna'i (La-*na*-i), once-desolate island home of evil spirits

mahalo (ma-*ha*-lo), thank you

maika (*mai*-ka), bowling game played with stone discs

maile (*mai*-le), vine with fragrant leaves used for lei to show special honor

Mākolea (Ma-ko-*le*-a), chiefess, wife of Paka

malo (*ma*-lo), loincloth of kapa

māmane (ma-*ma*-ne), strong wood used for sled runners

mamo (*ma*-mo), glossy black bird with small tufts of golden feathers prized
   for royal featherwork

Maui (*Mau*-i), trickster hero; island from which Ka-ulu was banished

mea i pohō (*me*-a *i* po-*ho*), the loser

Moana-lua (Mo-*a*-na-*lu*-a), a section of O'ahu

Mokuola (*Mo*-ku-o-la), island of refuge

Mckila (Me-*ki*-la), handsome; warrior who became Riddler on the Hill

Ni'ihau (Ni-i-*hau*), desolate island beyond Kaua'i; early home of evil spirits

O'ahu (O-*a*-hu), island given to Paka of Hawai'i

'Ōla'a (O-*la*-a), village in Puna district of Hawai'i

olonā (o-lo-*na*), very strong cord made from bark of a shrub

Olopana (O-lo-*pa*-na), the High Chief slain by Kamapua'a

'ōpclu (o-*pe*-lu), silvery fish protected by strict kapu seasons

'ōpū (o-*pu*), stomach

'ōpū nui (o-*pu nu*-i), big stomach

Pā'eli (Pa-*e*-li), wise man of Moana-lua

pa'i ā pa'i (*pa*-i a *pa*-i), tied score

Paka (*Pa*-ka), youth who recovered his wife by answering a riddle

Pāka'alana (Pa-ka-a-*la*-na), sacred temple in Waipi'o Valley

poi (*po*-i), staple food of Hawaiians; made from taro root pounded to a paste

pola (*po*-la), platform of double canoe

pūhala (pu-*ha*-la), tree whose fruit was said to vanquish spirits

Puna (*Pu*-na), a district on Hawai'i; once ruled by Riddling Chief

Punia (Pu-*ni*-a), trickster who outwitted the Shark King

Pūpū (*Pu*-pu), young spearsman who won food for the people of Kohala

uhi-uhi (*u*-hi-*u*-hi), very hard wood used for sled runners

Waipi'o (Wai-*pi*-o), valley on island of Hawai'i

Wakaina (Wa-*kai*-na), the spirit who danced

wili-wili (*wi*-li-*wi*-li), lightweight wood used for surfboards and floats on
   outrigger canoes

Bibliography

Beckwith, Martha W. *Hawaiian Mythology.* Honolulu: University of Hawaii Press, 1970; "Hawaiian Riddles and Proverbs," *Friend* (Honolulu), Feb. 1932; "Hawaiian Riddling," *American Anthropologist*, 24:311–331, 1922.

Buck, Peter H. *Arts and Crafts of Hawaii.* Honolulu: Bishop Museum Press, 1957.

Elbert, Samuel H. *Selections from Fornander's Hawaiian Antiquities and Folklore.* Honolulu: University of Hawaii Press, 1959.

Fornander, Abraham. *An Account of the Polynesian Race.* 3 vols. Rutland, Vt.: Charles E. Tuttle Co., Inc. reprint, 1969; *Collection of Hawaiian Antiquities and Folklore.* 3 vols. Milwood, N.Y.: Kraus Reprint Co., 1974.

Green, Laura S. *Folktales from Hawaii.* Poughkeepsie: Vassar College Press, 1928.

Handy, E. S. Craighill, and others. *Ancient Hawaiian Civilization.* Rutland, Vt.: Charles E. Tuttle Co., Inc., rev. ed. 1965.

Judd, Henry P. "Hawaiian Proverbs and Riddles," *Bishop Museum Bulletin* (Honolulu), No. 77, 1930.

Luomala, Katharine, "Maui-of-a-Thousand-Tricks," *Bishop Museum Bulletin* (Honolulu), No. 198, 1949; *Voices on the Wind.* Honolulu: Bishop Museum Press, 1955.

Malo, David. *Hawaiian Antiquities.* Honolulu: Bishop Museum Press, 1951.

McAllister, J. Gilbert. "Archeology of Oahu," *Bishop Museum Bulletin* (Honolulu), No. 104:91–92, 1933.

Nakuina, Emma Metcalf. *Hawaii, Its People, Their Legends.* Honolulu: Hawaii Promotion Commission, 1904.

Neal, Marie C. *In Gardens of Hawaii.* Honolulu: Bishop Museum Press, 1965.

Pratt, Helen Gay. *The Hawaiians, an Island People.* New York: Charles Scribner's Sons, 1941.

Pukui, Mary Kawena and Elbert, Samuel H. *Hawaiian Dictionary*, revised edition. Honolulu: University of Hawaii Press, 1986.

Rice, William Hyde. "Hawaiian Legends," *Bishop Museum Bulletin* (Honolulu), No. 3:7–137, 1923.

Stokes, John F. G. *Index to an Account of the Polynesian Race.* Honolulu: Bishop Museum Press, 1909.

Thrum, Thomas G. *More Hawaiian Folktales.* Chicago: A. C. McClurg & Co., 1923.

Westervelt, W. D. *Legends of Maui, a Demigod of Polynesia.* Honolulu: Hawaiian Gazette Co., Ltd., 1910; *Hawaiian Legends of Old Honolulu.* Rutland, Vt.: Charles E. Tuttle Co., Inc., 1963.